S0-BAD-365

DISCARD

CHICAGO PUBLIC LIBRARY
BEVERLY BRANCH
1962 W. 95TH STREET
CHICAGO, IL 60643

THE BEST
AMERICAN
SHORT PLAYS

2000–2001

CHICAGO PUBLIC LIBRARY
BEVERLY BRANCH
1962 W. 95TH STREET
CHICAGO, IL 60643

CHICAGO PUBLIC LIBRARY
BEVERLY BRANCH
2121 W 95TH ST. 60643

Best American Short Plays Series

The Best American Short Plays

2000–2001

edited by

Mark Glubke

CHICAGO PUBLIC LIBRARY
BEVERLY BRANCH
1962 W. 95TH STREET
CHICAGO, IL 60643

An Applause Original

THE BEST AMERICAN SHORT PLAYS 2000-2001

No part of this publication may be reproduced or transmitted in any form or by any means, electronic or mechanical, including photocopy, recording, or any information storage or retrieval system now known to be invented, without permission in writing from the publishers, except by a reviewer who wishes to quote brief passages in connection with a review written for inclusion in a magazine, newspaper or broadcast.

NOTE: All plays contained in this volume are fully protected under the Copyright Laws of the United States of America, the British Empire, including the Dominion of Canada, and all other countries of the International Copyright Union and the Universal Copyright Convention. Permission to reproduce, wholly or in part, by any method, must be obtained from the copyright owners or their agents. (See CAUTION notices at the beginning of each play.)

Copyright © 2002 by Applause Theatre & Cinema Books
All Rights Reserved
ISBN 1-55783-480-6 (cloth), 1-55783-481-4 (paper)
ISSN 0067-6284

APPLAUSE THEATRE & CINEMA BOOKS
151 West 46th Street, 8th Floor
New York, NY 10036
Phone: (212) 575-9265
Fax: (646) 562-5852
Email: info@applausepub.com
Internet: www.applausepub.com

SALES & DISTRIBUTION

North America:
HAL LEONARD CORP.
7777 West Bluemound Road
P. O. Box 13819
Milwaukee, WI 53213
Phone: (414) 774-3630
Fax: (414) 774-3259
Email: halinfo@halleonard.com
Internet: www.halleonard.com

UK:
COMBINED BOOK SERVICES LTD.
Units I/K, Paddock Wood Distribution Centre
Paddock Wood, Tonbridge, Kent TN12 6UU
Phone: (44) 01892 837171
Fax: (44) 01892 837272
United Kingdom

Interior design by Mulberry Tree Press, Inc (www.mulberrytreepress.com)

Printed in Canada

R01901 32149

CONTENTS

CHICAGO PUBLIC LIBRARY
BEVERLY BRANCH
1962 W. 95TH STREET
CHICAGO, IL 60643

CHICAGO PUBLIC LIBRARY
BEVERLY BRANCH
2121 W 95TH ST   60643

This anthology is dedicated to Horton Foote,
who continues to provide matchless inspiration,
both as an artist and as a man

CHICAGO PUBLIC LIBRARY
BEVERLY BRANCH
1962 W. 95TH STREET
CHICAGO, IL 60643

CHICAGO PUBLIC LIBRARY
BEVERLY BRANCH
2121 W 95TH ST   60643

ACKNOWLEDGMENTS

FOR SHARING THEIR KNOWLEDGE of these writers with me, I am indebted to Stephen Willems, literary manager at MCC Theater, playwrights Gary Sunshine and Liz Duffy Adams, and agents Ron Gwiazda and Mary Harden. This volume would not have been possible without your invaluable help.

INTRODUCTION

A FEW YEARS BACK, I heard the great playwright Terrence McNally deliver a lecture in which he encouraged writers to "write plays that matter. Raise the stakes. Shout, yell, holler, but make yourself heard. It's time for playwrights to reclaim the theater. We do that by speaking from the heart about the things that matter most to us."

Of late, we find ourselves in a world so filled with rage that the very definition of violence has had to be modified to include previously unimaginable acts. Suddenly, there's an ever greater need for artists to speak from the heart about the things that matter. Suddenly there's a renewed need for authentic voices to challenge us, frighten us, inspire us, even transform us. As always, there remains a need for voices simply to entertain, to help us laugh in the face of pain with childlike abandon.

Tennessee Williams once referred to artists as the "nervous system of any age or nation." I rather like that analogy and feel strongly that the nervous system in this age—at least as it pertains to theater—appears to be functioning just fine. I might even go so far as to say it's thriving. There are those, of course, who pass their days insisting theater has outlived any usefulness, that it's dying a death that's slow and painful but not unmerited. While the naysayers eagerly pursue their deathbed vigil (most likely home alone evenings at eight), I attend shows and am heartened by the thrilling new voices I encounter everywhere. These aren't writers moonlighting from screen, TV or novel writing, they're talented writers writing specifically for the stage. They're playwrights.

In this latest edition of a prestigious series dating back more than sixty years, I'm proud to introduce a handful of these writers. Included in *The Best American Short Plays* for the first time, each possesses a distinctive voice. Each has something important to say. Each is poised to have a formidable impact on theater in the new century.

In *Poodle with Guitar and Dark Glasses* Liz Duffy Adams introduces us to five characters: a romance novelist, a painter, an activist, a teacher and a photographer. On its surface, the play is whimsical, absurd and very, very funny. However, a closer look reveals a chaotic world with a dissonant undertow. Though frustrated, each character is struggling to push through desperation toward authenticity and some sort of personal Nirvana. Jade, the painter, comments to her dog, "This is something much much bigger than a dog portrait. Bigger than my cash commission. Even bigger than art. This has to do with some kind of, uh, mystical transcendent zeitgeist kind of thing." Some similar kind of, uh, thing can be said of Adams' play.

Glen Berger, familiar to many of us from his acclaimed New York production of *Underneath the Lintel*, is represented here with *I Will Go...I Will Go*. Inspired by the true story of Henry Sullivan, who in 1923 became the first American to swim the English Channel, it's a simple, evocatively told tale of perseverance. Henry's fortitude is tempered, however, by the simmering pathos of unrequited love. There's also undeniable poignancy in Sullivan's explanation to the press of why he's endangering his life: "Should I make it, even at the end of the century. . . they will remember me." We in the audience realize, of course, that he was not remembered. Until Berger's play, that is.

A man attempts suicide by throwing himself off a bridge and instead lands on top of a woman. Thus begins Benjamin Bettenbender's darkly humorous *The Siren Song of Stephen Jay Gould*. The new acquaintances (both characters unnamed) swan dive instantly into an intimate conversation, covering everything from science and love to sex and the seemingly arbitrary nature of life. Though they move slowly from despair toward hope, the journey is fortified by a delicious sense of humor. "You might want to try a bigger bridge the next time," the woman says. "I would, but this is the only one around," the man responds. "Heck, go somewhere," the woman suggests. "Drive down to New York. They have lots of bridges there. You could get a hotel, see a show. Make a weekend of it."

Quirky comedy with an absurdist twist is a specialty of Cusi Cram, a writer I first encountered in 1999 via her New York production of *Landlocked*. In *West of Stupid*, she transports us to a sidewalk cafe in the Campo di Fiori section of Rome. A mother and son are conversing. At first this appears a simple comedy in which the outspoken mother makes embarrassingly blunt sexual references interspersed with broad generalizations. "Are there no large, poetic and philosophical people in the entire state of the Connecticut, Mother?" the son asks, angrily. "In my opinion," she replies, "very few." Yet, as the conversation continues, we're led into surprisingly vulnerable territory, territory where issues such as mortality and the mystical bond between mother and child come to the fore.

In Laurence Klavan's *The Summer Sublet* we're thrust into a world of voyeurism, sexual obsession and danger. Lloyd sublets an apartment where he's frightened by wildly violent and abusive fighting between a husband and wife in the apartment below. Convinced the woman's life is in danger, Lloyd meets her and is drawn, almost immediately and helplessly, into an erotic relationship. It's an affair that puts Lloyd's life in danger and leads to a shattering, unexpected, climax. Featured in Ensemble Studio Theatre's 24th Annual Festival of One-Act Plays, *The Summer Sublet* is an eerie, cautionary tale that haunts the mind long after the curtain descends.

Deep compassion and a palpable sense of loss charge Seth Kramer's *World Without Memory*. Thirtysomething Robin is dining with Abe, her septuagenarian father. Abe reminisces lovingly about his late wife, particularly the times they went fishing. "There is nothing, never has been never will be, that can taste like those days on Lake Oka-Bodgi with your mother," he says. Robin notices, however, that Abe's having a little trouble following the conversation, having trouble remembering, having trouble finding words. In the nine short scenes that follow, Robin slowly, heartbreakingly loses her father to Alzheimer's. *World Without Memory* is an achingly humane play that explores several issues at the core of the human condition: aging, mortality and the passage of time.

"Henry set me free. He really did. Now maybe I can fall in love again. He came to me in a dream . . . came rowing over in a red, scruffy boat." Thus begins Rosemary Moore's lyrical and poignant monologue *The Pain Of Pink Evenings*. It introduces us to Tracy Lusk, a woman on the cusp of middle age, speaking from "a state of epiphany." A widow for ten years, Tracy clings to the memory of her dead husband. Then he appears to her, saying, "I've come to say good-bye. It's been ten years since I died and you mustn't think of me anymore. I know you are struggling and I want something good for you." It's a vision that pushes Tracy beyond the shadow of grief, into the light of self-discovery and, ultimately, freedom.

In Julie Marie Myatt's *What He Sent (Photos from Brooklyn)* we visit with a likable young photographer named Billy. As he sets up his equipment for a photo shoot, he narrates a slide show that depicts the last three years of his life. With tremendous humor, he tells us about forging a new identity in New York City, getting a job, losing a job, falling in love, getting married and more. Though a series of largely unremarkable events, the vignettes add up to a whole that captures the angst, the wonder, the uncertainty and the potential of urban life at the beginning of the 21st century. Billy's fortitude is summed up in his first description, of a blurry photo of New York: "June 1998. If I can make it here, I'll make it anywhere. (The 'it' remains shaky. But the 'I' arrives hopeful.)"

In recognition of his critically acclaimed work at the American Repertory Theatre over the past two years, playwright and novelist Adam Rapp has been hailed as "the hot talent of the moment" (*The Boston Herald*). In his powerful *Train Story*, a middle-aged book editor is traveling cross-country by train from New York to Los Angeles. "At a stop in the Midwest, the doors part and let in the smell of oil refineries. The stench somehow venereal. Like whores on the subway. A young girl enters from the adjacent car. She might be eighteen, nineteen. She holds a paper bag containing a forty-ounce bottle of beer. She has eyes like bullet holes. Nothing but pupil. She starts asking around for drugs." As these two very different women traverse the continent, so do they cover the considerably more hazardous, and vaster, terrain of the soul. By the end of the trip, through circumstances neither could have foreseen, these women will be deeply, painfully connected in ways they, and you, will never forget.

Abandonment and death cast a wide shadow over Brian Silberman's deeply imaginative play *Walkin' Backward*. Set in a small back-country Virginia town in 1965, it's the story of three teenage boys running away from home. The central figure, 13-year-old Cooney Webster, buried his mom earlier that day and is now an orphan. Walking along a set of decrepit train tracks, the trio is ostensibly headed for the site of a famous Civil War train wreck. In actuality, their walk leads them to painful truths about their parents, and directs them to make some kind of sense of the chaos and pain in their young lives. *Walkin' Backward*, along with a related play titled *The Gospel According to Toots Pope*, received awards from Arena Stage, The American Alliance for Theater Education, the Kennedy Center, and The Poets' Theatre, among others.

In *Al Takes a Bride*, Gary Sunshine sweeps us back to 19th century Memphis for a lyrical tale of forbidden love. Alice Mitchell and Freda Ward, both 19, have fallen in love and, on a riverbank before the setting sun, are fantasizing about getting married. "I can see myself in this beautiful dress," says Freda, "my face as white as lilies, my hair a sunburst beaming down to my train, my waist a tiny halo, sculpted upward toward my softness, wrapped tight and secure, peeking out to my chin, which has never stood prouder, never lovelier." But *Al Takes a Bride* is more than a sweet love story. It speaks volumes about the role imagination plays in our lives. As the story reaches its surprising tragic climax, it also examines what can happen when hope is lost.

I met up with Sheri Wilner's work four years ago at Louisville's Humana Festival of New American Plays. In *Relative Strangers*, she introduces us to two strangers, both named Marie but a generation apart in age, seated together on a flight from New York to Charleston. As they talk, the younger woman decides the older woman beside her could be the mother she never had. "I know you must think I am a weirdo, but I'm not. I don't have a mother, you see. It's something I'm aware of every second of the day. Like if I didn't have any arms or legs . . . or skin. She died during childbirth. They say as soon as I emerged—as soon as I took my first breath—she took her last. She really was only a vessel for me if you think about it —just like this plane. She received me, took me to a destination and then I emerged, disembarked and she was gone. Lame metaphor, I know, but the mind—my mind—needs ways to understand, to make sense. I'm always feeling so…lost—like everyone in the world has a map that I don't have." *Relative Strangers*, by turns poignant and hilarious, brilliantly captures our universal longing for deeper connection and understanding.

Twelve writers. Twelve distinct voices. Twelve very different stories that make us smile, that shock us into reality (and, on occasion, unreality), that make us uncomfortable and that sometimes haunt our sleep. But as they challenge us in their myriad ways, they all equally succeed, Mr. McNally, at speaking from the heart about the things that matter.

MARK GLUBKE
New York City
February 2002

POODLE WITH GUITAR AND DARK GLASSES

A Rhapsody in Four Brief Acts

Liz Duffy Adams

For Gail, my mother

Poodle with Guitar and Dark Glasses by Liz Duffy Adams. Copyright © 1994 by Liz Duffy Adams. All rights reserved. Reprinted by permission of the author.

CAUTION: Professionals and amateurs are hereby warned that *Poodle with Guitar and Dark Glasses* by Liz Duffy Adams is subject to a royalty. It is fully protected under the copyright laws of the United States of America, and of all countries covered by the International Copyright Union (including the Dominion of Canada and the rest of the British Commonwealth), and of all countries covered by the Pan-American Copyright Convention and the Universal Copyright Convention, and of all countries with which the United States has reciprocal copyright relations. All rights, including professional, amateur, motion picture, recitation, lecturing, public reading, radio broadcasting, television, video or sound taping, all other forms of mechanical or electronic reproduction, such as information storage and retrieval systems and photo-copyright, and the rights of translation into foreign languages are strictly reserved. Particular emphasis is laid upon the question of readings, permission for which must be secured from the author or her agent in writing.

All inquiries concerning performance rights should be addressed to Liz Duffy Adams, c/o Applause Theatre & Cinema Books, 151 West 46th Street, 8th Floor, New York, N.Y. 10036.

Liz Duffy Adams

LIZ DUFFY ADAMS' plays include *Dog Act* (staged readings at Portland Stage Company's Little Festival of the Unexpected 2000 and New York Theater Workshop, Finalist for the Clauder Competition 2001); *The Train Play* (a Clubbed Thumb production at Ohio Theater, Finalist for the Clauder Competition 1999); *A Wrinkle in Time* (adaptation commissioned and produced by Syracuse Stage); *A Fabulous Beast* (One Dream Theater); *Teacup for a Shallow Apocalypse* (Santa Monica Playhouse); and the short plays *Greeks & Centaurs*, *The Last Woman on Earth*, and *Aphra Does Antwerp* (The Women's Project Tandem Acts Festivals; *Last Woman* also at New Georges Perform-a-thon 2000 and Estrogenius 2001). She is a graduate of NYU's Experimental Theater Wing and the Yale School of Drama, and a member of New Dramatists.

CHARACTERS

> FUCHSIA, romance novelist
> JADE, painter
> VIOLET, community activist
> GRAY, ESL teacher
> JERRY, photographer

> *They are all out of their first youth, at least.*

TIME & SETTING

> A few years ago. Five tiny studios above an after-hours club in an urban art slum. Between midnight and 4 A.M. on four consecutive nights.

Note: *the Russian text is spelled phonetically. English translations are provided in parentheses, not to be spoken.*

ACT 1

[FUCHSIA *sitting at a desk with a container of coffee, a tape recorder, cigarettes, in an otherwise bare room. A single bare lightbulb overhead. She presses the record button.*]

FUCHSIA: *Carnival Desire* by Fuchsia deMornay, chapter three. Deserine walked pensively out onto the dark, deserted pier. In the distance she could hear the gay music of the fairground, and the carefree laughter of happy people, but the sounds only made her feel more lonely. She wrapped her slender, tanned arms around herself, and felt tears welling up in her large almond-shaped, emerald-green eyes. "Deserine duPrey," she thought fiercely, "you just stop feeling sorry for yourself! So what if the only man you've ever loved is a no-good, lying, cheating scoundrel who probably never loved you at all..." Against her will, her heartbroken tears poured down her lovely face, and her slender tanned shoulders shook with—uh, scratch that—her, uh, her delicate, tawny shoulders shook with the sobs she couldn't hold back any longer. Suddenly she felt a man's strong hands on her shoulders, and without looking she knew it was him. She'd know his touch anywhere. But she knew she could not surrender to it, not this time. "Go away, Brett! Just leave me alone!" Behind her, he murmured, "Deserine, please tell me what's wrong. Let me help." His deep, masculine voice held a note of puzzled concern that sounded so sincere, it sent a stab of doubt through Deserine's heart. But she pushed it firmly away. She wasn't going to be made a fool of, not again! She whirled around, auburn curls dancing, and faced him. "Brett Bronco," she cried, "you can just suck my dick!" A subversive thrill swept through her—

[FUCHSIA *stops the tape. She rewinds, plays back: "'Brett Bronco,' she cried, 'you can just suck my dick!'" She stops the tape, lights a cigarette. Smokes in silence for a moment, looking into space. She rewinds the tape slightly and plays back the line "'Brett Bronco,' she cried." She stops the tape, then hits record and continues.*]

"I, I never want to see you again! Do you hear me? Never!" She choked back a sob, and stumbled past him towards the safety of the fairground. She knew if he touched her again she would be lost.

[*Lights down on* FUCHSIA, *up on* JADE's *studio. There is a stool or table holding paints and a jar full of brushes, and an easel that holds a small white canvas. She is talking to a Polaroid photograph.*]

JADE: OK, Blini. Time to be immortalized. You may think you're just a rich happy poodle, insofar as you do think, just a lap dog in the lap of luxury, but when I get through with you, you'll be art, baby, A, R, T; art with a capital ARF! [*Bark.*] Yeah, yeah, OK, dog portraiture is a little degrading, but the wolf's at the door, know what I mean, Blini? Yeah. One dog portrait, two months rent. Bite the dog biscuit, Jade. Wake up and smell the kibble.

[*She clips the Polaroid to the easel.*]

Hey, listen. In times past there was no shame in portraiture for pay. In having a patron you flattered for a fee. Royalty, nobility, the just plain rich. So now it's dogs. So what's the difference? Everyone knows dogs are more noble than people anyway. Everyone knows that loyalty, devotion, faithfulness and courage are now exclusively canine virtues. [*Slight pause.*] Good dog.

[*She puts a cassette into a tape player on the floor; we hear Elvis Presley's "Hound Dog." She begins painting. Lights down on her, up on* VIOLET, *sitting at a table in her own bleak cell. There's a telephone, a notebook, a pen. The phone on the table rings; she picks up.*]

VIOLET: Neighborhood Action Help-line, this is Violet... Oh, no, we don't do AIDS testing here, we're not a clinic. But I can give a referral... A number. I can give you a number to call. For a clinic. OK, the number is 634-2468. Ask for Sandy, she'll take care of you. OK. Good luck.

[*She hangs up. Writes in notebook, murmuring:*]

Woman, AIDS test referral, Sandy.

[*The phone rings. She picks up.*]

Neighborhood Action Help-line, this is Violet. Uh, no, we don't do pregnancy tests, we're not a clinic. But I can give you the—hello?

[*She hangs up. Writes in notebook:*]

Pregnancy test, incomplete referral.

[*Phone rings. She picks up.*]

Neighborhood Action Help-line, Violet. Oh, housing, yes, housing's tricky right now, there's a freeze on Section Eights, and there are hardly any low income units available in the neighborhood except for units being illegally warehoused. But I can give you a number to call. Ready? 899-3579, talk to Naomi, she can tell you where else to call. What? Oh. Oh no. No, I don't have any room in my apartment. I'm sor—Oh, I'm sure your kids are quiet and everything, I just, I'm sorry, I don't have room. It's, it's a studio. I'm sorry but...Where are you now, in the...? Oh, uh huh, the shelter. I know. I know. It's bad, I know. Look, you talk to Naomi. OK? You hang in there. Call me again if you want to talk about it. OK? OK.

[*She hangs up. Starts to write in notebook but the phone rings again.*]

Neighborhood Action Help-line, Violet. Oh, uh, por favor, slowly, señora, mi español es no muy bueno. ¿Que? No comprendo. ¿Que? Oh, oh, OK. Neccessitas llamar ocho nueve nueve, tres cinco siete nueve, hablas a Naomi. Sí. Sí. ¿Que? Oh, no. No. No, mi casa es muy, um, poquita, yo no tengo...uh, lo siento, hablas a Naomi, ¿sí? Sí. No problema. Buen, buenas noches.

[*Hangs up. Phone rings. She picks up.*]

Neighborhood Action Help-line, Violet...Hello?...Hello?...Is someone there?...Hello?...Can I help you?...Can I help you?

[*The lights down on her, up on* GRAY *facing the audience. He speaks slowly and clearly, with emphasis on the to-be verb.*]

GRAY: My name is Gray. What is your name? [*Pause.*] Hello. My name is Gray. What is your name? What is your name? Hello. My name is Gray. What is your name? Is your name Ivan? Listen. His name is Ivan. What is his name? His name is Ivan. Good. What is your name? My name is Gray. What is your name? Good. My name is Gray. I am a teacher. Are you a student? Yes, you are a student. Listen. You are a student. Am I a teacher? Yes, I am a teacher. Good. Is my name Gray? Yes, my name is Gray. Listen. My name is Gray. I am in despair. Are you in despair? Is he in despair? Am I in despair? Good. Good. Class dismissed.

[*The lights cross-fade back to* VIOLET. *The phone rings; she answers.*]

VIOLET: Neighborhood Action Help-line, Violet...What? The birds are flying south? What do you mean? I don't understand. Hello?

[*She hangs up. Writes in notebook:*]

Unidentifiable person, reporting bird migration. No referral.

[*Phone rings. She answers.*]

Neighborhood Action, the birds are flying south...I'm sorry, what?... Oh. I'm sorry, I can't help you. I have no number for you to call. I can't help you.

[*She hangs up. Writes in notebook:*]

Man, asking about my underwear. No referral.

[*Phone rings. She picks up.*]

Neighborhood, Violet, time to fly south. Don't call for help. Stock up on grubs. Fluff up and jettison your bone marrow.

[*She hangs up. Phone rings. She picks up.*]

A feather lands at my feet. I think about my mother. Long ago there was a fire and I became an orphan just like everybody else. Trajectory! Know your vector!

[*She hangs up. The phone rings. She whistles a bird call in response. Phone rings repeatedly, she answering each ring with a bird call. Lights down on her, up on* GRAY *in his cubicle, with* JERRY. *He pours a glass of bourbon, hands it to* JERRY, *who doesn't drink, pours himself a glass.*]

GRAY: I have a secret sorrow. What time is it? We really only have until about 4 A.M. That's when Rescue the Android opens up downstairs. The after-hours club. And the music starts. Around 4. It's very loud. I really can't complain. That's why this place is so cheap. It's supposed to be a studio. Commercial. I'm not supposed to live here. Well, I don't exactly live here. I sleep here. I keep my stuff in a box here. All my stuff. I don't have any stuff anywhere else. So I guess this is home. Home is where your stuff is. The super told me you're setting up a darkroom. I guess you're a photographer then. [*He doesn't seem to expect a response.*] I guess he's the super. Or something. We pay the rent to him. Maybe he's the landlord. Probably he's nobody and it's some kind of a racket and we're all trespassing and could be thrown out anytime right into the street. I teach English as a Second Language. Does that sound interesting? It's not. After a day in there, everywhere I go these horrible sentences are running through my mind. Where are you from? Are you from Russia? Are you in America now? What is your name? And over and over again I hear "my name Galina." Or "I from Russia." They don't have the "to be" verb in Russian. That's what I'm told. I don't actually speak Russian. But do you believe that? I don't understand it. I guess they've got some kind of a way of thinking about it, but no direct equivalent. It drives them nuts. They say, "English stupid language." Which, oddly enough, infuriates me. I mean, it's kind of ludicrous. What do I care? So, the secret. I don't know. Why should I tell you? I don't really know you. I don't know you at all. There's no reason to think you'd be interested. Why should you be interested? Who the hell are you anyway? Some low-life photographer. Renting a darkroom on Avenue B, you're probably some pornographer or something. Not that I'd object to that. I like the idea of pornography. It means people care about something, somebody cares about something somewhere, even if it's just sex or money. Which is pornography? Sex or money? Who knows, right? I think I used to care about sex and money, stuff like that, but now all I care about is getting a bunch of stupid fucking Russians to say I am. You are. He fucking is.

[*Lights up on* FUCHSIA. *She's lying on her back on the desk, cigarette in her mouth, tape recorder on her stomach.*]

FUCHSIA: Chapter six. Deserine whirled around in front of the big mirror, admiring herself in her wedding dress, her tiny waist snugly encased in white satin. "It's perfect!," she cried to the fitter. "I'm so happy! It's like a dream!" As the fitter began to undo the dozens of tiny satin buttons down her back, she fell into a happy reverie. Who would have dreamed that she, Deserine duPrey, a nobody, an orphan without any family, would end up marrying Brett Bronco, the most eligible bachelor in the state! Handsome, dashing, rich and ambitious, desired by every woman he met! And he was all hers! Or would be, in only a few days, when the minister would say, "I now pronounce you..." Deserine felt an inexplicable twinge of nausea. [FUCHSIA *moves the tape recorder off her stomach and rolls up onto one elbow as she continues.*] As the fitter bore away the gleaming cloud of satin, Deserine stood musing in her slip. What was this gnawing little feeling of doubt? Suddenly, as if summoned by her thoughts, Brett stood in the doorway. "Brett!" she gasped, a pretty pink blush rising in her cheeks, "You shouldn't be in here!" Brett strode forward and enveloped her in his arms, a cocky grin on his lips. "Don't I have the right to be with the woman who's about to become Mrs. Brett Bronco?" "That's Ms. duPrey to you, buddy!" Deserine was startled. Had that come out of her mouth? She knew perfectly well that this was where she was supposed to melt into Brett's arms. What was the matter with her? Brett was clearly shaken, but made a manly attempt to get them back on track. With a deep chuckle, he nuzzled her neck and said, "Well now, you can call yourself anything you want to, as long as you remember that you're my girl!" Deserine pushed him away. Amazed, she heard herself say, "Jeez, Brett, do you ever listen to yourself?" Brett was stunned: "What are you talking about?" "Well, come on. Do we always have to stay with the script? Does everything have to be so formulaic?" Brett was getting a little pissed off. "Hey, Deserine, the formula works. Girl meets boy, girl hates boy although feeling physically attracted to him, there is a major obstacle that is revealed to be based on a complete misunderstanding, girl gets boy, meaning there is a proposal of marriage or an implicit understanding of one, girl is thrilled to the marrow by boy's kiss, or by his sexual technique, depending on the market. What more do you need?" [*Slight pause.*] Deserine was impressed by the clarity of his vision.

[FUSCHIA *stops the tape. Lights up on* VIOLET. *The phone rings. She picks up.*]

VIOLET: Rock. Sky. Conflagration. Rescue. Shelter. Sanctuary. Eat. Drink. Hover. Land. Water. Multitudes. Flap. Flap. Flap. Fish. Bugs. Bones. Salt. Blood. Brine. Aerodynamics. Wind. Wet. Fellows. Magnetic Poles. Rise. Rise. Currents. Streams. Navigation. Night. Moon. Sleep. Warm. Soar. Light. Heat. Direction. Up. Up. Arc. Vector. Vector. Vector.

[*She hangs up. Lights up on* JADE *looking at her canvas with brush in hand. The half-finished painting is of a poodle wearing a flashy white jumpsuit.*]

JADE: Uh oh.

[*Suddenly, very loud music starts pumping up from the after-hours club downstairs. The four of them stop what they're doing and leave. A red light comes up on* JERRY *who is developing pictures in his darkroom. Projected large we see photographs of* FUCHSIA, JADE, VIOLET *and* GRAY, *obviously taken recently and surreptitiously. In the red glow* JERRY *dances in place to the music, dips photos in trays, hangs them on a clothesline. This goes on for a minute. Then simultaneously: the music stops abruptly,* JERRY'*s light goes out and lights go up on the next night:*]

ACT 2

FUCHSIA: Deserine dropped the turbo into third gear and took another slug of Colt 45. "I know this is wrong, oh so wrong," she mused, one of her pearly perfect teeth pressing into her full lower lip. "But it feels so good." Tying and gagging Brett and dumping him in the back seat of his own Corvette was wrong too, she knew that. She coaxed the speedometer past ninety-five, cracked the window and let the sharp night air fill her lungs. "I don't know, Brett. I thought I believed in the formula. After all, it was what I knew. But lately, I can't say why, I've been having doubts. I mean, gee, if you think about it, what is romance but a biological scam? It's nature's little way of tricking a girl into letting a guy get close enough to impregnate her. Really. If it weren't for love, who'd ever get pregnant? It's not exactly its own reward. I mean, it's disfiguring, painful, and potentially fatal. Yikes. So, you can understand, the way I'm feeling about all this, well, I just have to think this through before I take any chances. OK, Brett, honey?" A muffled curse from the back seat was her only answer. Deserine sighed, tossed back the last of the malt liquor, and eased the 'vette onto the exit ramp. It was time to hit the back roads.

[FUCHSIA *hits the stop button on her tape recorder, reaches for her coffee and cigarettes. Lights up on* GRAY *in his classroom.*]

GRAY: Hello. My name is Gray. What is your name? What is your name? Is your name Sergei? My name Gray. Your name Sergei? Good. I from New York. Where you from? You from Moscow? Good. You from Moscow. I teacher. You teacher? No? You student? Yes, you student. Where Yelena from? Yelena from Minsk? Good. Yelena, Yelena from Minsk. You married? Yes, you married. Good. Good. She married? No, she not married. She, she single. Vladimir married? Yes, Vladimir, uh, Vladimir...married...Good. I, I, uh, I not married. I, single. You... uh, he...uh, she...I, I, I...

[*He stands with his mouth open, searching. Lights up on* JADE. *The unfinished Poodle in Jumpsuit has been joined by a somewhat larger unfinished Poodle with Guitar and Dark Glasses. There is a fresh, even larger canvas on the easel.*]

JADE: OK, Blini, my friend. No more kidding around. Mama needs a shit-load of art supplies. OK? This is it. I mean it. We're gonna paint your goddamn portrait just like we're supposed to. You're just a poodle. Right? Not the incarnation of some dead and buried rock star. You got that? I mean it this time. Just. A. Poodle.

[She raises her paint brush, advances on the canvas. Lights up on VIOLET. *She is standing on her desk, arms outstretched as if soaring. Occasionally she flaps leisurely. She is very high up, migrating. Lights up on* FUCHSIA, *talking to* JERRY.]*

FUCHSIA: I'm very confused, it's out of my hands, she's completely out of my control and where does that leave me? and you know romance used to be so simple to me, just a meal ticket but suddenly everything's being called into question, like can anyone explain to me the difference or boundary or link or dichotomy or what-have-you of love and sex, you know, romance vs. lust, I mean is there an issue there or is it just semantics or, you know, a matter of lighting: sharp focus is sex, soft focus is romance? not useful distinctions maybe but you know what do I know? haven't had sex in, Christ, years, mainly I suppose because I'm *just terrified*, naturally; who are all these people who are fucking as if it's *harmless*, are they not paying attention? and anyway I never can decide who it is, you know, who it is that I desire, it feels like all or nothing, I mean like I could want *absolutely everybody*, male, female, young, old, just be utterly pansexual and have a carnal experience with every creature I encounter or else shut it down and forget where I left the key, you know, not even get started, because it's that middle ground where all those distinctions have to be made, all those evaluations and choices, that I personally find just *too much*. I don't know why I'm telling you all this. I don't really know you. I don't know you at all. I hear you're a photojournalist or something. I bet that's interesting. Snatch yourself a hunk of what's happening and turn it into a paycheck. Or art. Which is photojournalism, money or art? I'm an orphan. I was separated from my family at a traveling fun fair and raised by kindly carneys. It was a good life. I have no regrets. I do sometimes wonder how I got here from there, you know what I mean? Like tonight. I was walking over here, around dusk. And I pass a couple screaming at each other on the sidewalk, just screaming in front of strangers and everything, and I'm kicking aside a discarded needle just as a couple of little kids run past me, playing, and it's all very comfortable and familiar in a way, the broken glass, the rubble-filled lots, the smell of sour wine as I pass a bar, and an ice cream truck comes cruising down the street, playing that little tune, you know? [*Imitates it.*] And I flashed on when I was a kid, in the carnival. Once in a while, if it started to rain, and there weren't any customers, the merry-go-round guys would keep it going for a while, and carneys who'd gotten caught in the rain away from their booths or trailers would jump on, you know, get out of the rain? And I'd be hanging onto my favorite horse, a really fierce black-maned stallion, and we'd be going around with the colored lights sparkling off the rain and the tinny old merry-go-round music playing and all those tough old carneys grinning and whooping except for the guys who were starting a card game in the swan-bench. [*Slight pause.*] I know there were a lot of steps in my life between then and now but for a moment I saw then and now side by side and it just did not make any sense at all.

[*Lights up on GRAY in his room, holding the bottle of bourbon. He shuts his eyes and struggles.*]

GRAY: I, I, I Gray. No. I, Gray. I, Gray! My name...Gray! *No*, oh, no, something missing, something, lost. What, who, what, I? I? Iiii? [*Slumps exhausted against the desk, takes a slug of bourbon. Tries again.*] You, you, you...We, we...They...Ohhh. [*Moans, drinks.*] I! I! I!!! She, oh, she... She...[*Weeping.*] She. She. Nothing. Gone. I. Nothing. Gone. Lost. [*Collapses into fetal position on the desk, sobbing. After a moment he says through his sobs:*] OH, yatak neshohslif. Shtota pateryana, shtota tak nushnaya minya...[*He stops crying, sits up and listens to himself.*] Padeshdi minutu.

(OH, I am so miserable. Something is missing, something so necessary to me...[*He stops crying, sits up and listens to himself.*] Wait a minute.)

[*Lights on VIOLET who is perched on her desk, singing:*]

VIOLET:
The sky is blue
The sky is pink
The sky is violet I think
The world is gray
The world is green

The world is something to be seen
I'd like to tell you all, my dears
All of my hopes, all of my fears
And about all the joy that hollow bones can give
But I hope you won't take offense
You see, it's simply too immense
The sense I've only just begun to live

Now that I've turned to flight
I am the queen of night
I navigate by starlight and by moon
There is no greater glee
Than mocking gravity
I only hope that dawn won't come too soon

When I look back at those
Bipedal days of old
Why did I take so long to take to wing?
Stumping around on earth
Was all I'd known since birth
I never realized that I could fling...!

[*Speaking:*]

Feathers keep you warm, bird thoughts are simple and few, that's the
way to be happy. Bird eyes see good colors, air flow takes you up, there's
science involved but you don't really have to think about it. I've got
a flock, of course, we flock together, we roost together in a tree.
Heads tucked under wings, tiny bird hearts racing, racing, pumping
warm and fast. It's time to head south. We're all flying south. We're
all flying south together. Time to go. Let's go. Here we go. We're going.
South. South. South.

[*The lights up on* JADE. *On the easel is a painting of a poodle in a sports car
with Ann-Margaret next to him, her blond hair flying. Jade is laying on the last
brush strokes. She turns away to wipe her brush on a rag, humming "Hound Dog" to
herself. The first two paintings are still in plain sight. She turns back, looks at
the painting. Stops humming. Stares. Softly:*]

JADE: Fuck me. [*Slight pause.*] Well, OK. OK, Blini. You can just wipe that curly-lipped smirk off that little muzzle of yours, because it ain't over yet. This ain't no heartbreak hotel. I want money, I need money, I love money, and no hard-headed poodle's gonna get in my way. You may as well just surrender. Oh, man. This is too much. I'm all shook up. Listen, Blini, don't be cruel. Won't you be my teddy-pooch? Huh? [*She moves the painting off the easel and puts a larger-yet blank canvas in its place, picks up her brush.*] It's now or never. My bills won't wait. And just a big-a big-a big-a hunk o' art will do.

[*Lights up on* FUCHSIA.]

FUCHSIA: Deserine stood naked by the motel window, watching the dawn come up over the desert. It was the most beautiful thing she'd ever seen. She felt something in her soul reach out and become one with the glow of sunlight at the horizon, with the desert and the flowering cacti. She even thought she might be having a spiritual epiphany. She wasn't sure. It was something she'd read about somewhere, maybe in Cosmo. She heard a faint snore behind her and turned around. Brett lay sprawled across the bed, fast asleep with his mouth slightly open. She contemplated him. Taken as a natural phenomenon, she had to admit he was easily as impressive as a desert sunrise. Not only that, as she'd just discovered, his sexual technique was thrilling to the marrow. It wasn't a spiritual epiphany, but it was pretty damned good. But where did all that leave her? Her entire existence had been in the service and pursuit of romance, and now she was forced to admit she really didn't know what love was. And she wasn't going to find out in this motel room. Deserine put her clothes on, left the car keys on the dresser and slipped quietly out the door. At the motel gift shop she bought bottled water and sun block, SPF 35. The desert was calling her. She had to go.

[*Lights up on* VIOLET *and* JERRY. *She's roosting on the edge of her desk.* JERRY *speaks in bird calls (translation provided in parentheses, not spoken).*]

JERRY: >>>>? (Where you headed?)

VIOLET: South.

JERRY: >>>>? (How come?)

VIOLET: It's a migratory thing. You wouldn't understand.

JERRY: >>>>>. >>>>>. >>>>>>? (But I'm interested. Explain it to me. What gets you going?)

VIOLET: Well. You get a feeling. It's hard to explain. You get restless. How it starts, you can't shut up. You chatter compulsively, chatter, chatter, chatter. Everybody else is feeling the same, everybody crowds together, chattering away: "what's happening-what's up-whaddaya wanna do-I dunno-I'm feelin' jumpy-how you feel-hey hey hey hey hey" and the noise of everybody chattering at once gets louder and louder and louder—this part can take days.

JERRY: >>>>>! (Sounds nerve-wracking!)

VIOLET: Oh, you bet. Next thing, you can't sit still. You start diving off your branch and swooping around and you don't know why. You feel like you're losing control, like there's this huge force that's pulling at you and you don't know what and you don't know where but you can't stay still. It's kind of exciting. Your heart's going bip-bip-bip-bip-bip, and you can't think at all, your mind's completely absent, you're just a singe focused burning sensation of *I gotta move*. And you're all feeling it together, you're all diving and swooping and chattering and with every dive and swoop you're getting more in sync, beginning more and more to move as one, drawing together from a ragged cloud of individuals into The Flock and it all comes together on an instant as you dive and instead of returning to the branches the swoop takes you back up and higher, higher, everyone finding their place in the formation—oh, you can't imagine what a feeling that is, to know your place in the formation—and you're off.

JERRY: >>>>>>>>>>? (Would you say you experience, oh, a certain clarity of purpose?)

VIOLET: Mmm. Yes. A clarity of purpose. Yes, I think that's part of it. There's no doubt, there are no questions. You don't have to think. It's really nice.

JERRY: >>>>>>? (But at the expense of the individual soul?)

VIOLET: The individual soul? What do you mean? I don't miss my sense of self, if that's what you mean. I don't have to make a lot of decisions. I don't have to fend for myself. I'm not out there struggling, anxious, lonely and confused like certain mammals I could name. You can keep your sense of self. I'll take the migrating flock. The flock takes care of its own. The flock sticks together. The flock is everything I need. [JERRY *leaves as she continues.*] It's good to be in the flock. To be a part of a large and complex whole. A perfectly placed detail of a beautiful pattern. Blissful communion. Exquisite mindlessness. Surrender the will. Drift with the wind. Soar with the flock. [*She looks upwards. The flock is gone. With increasing anxiety:*] Hey... guys? Hey, guys? Hey, guys!

[*The house music from Rescue the Android comes up very loud. All four continue what they're doing despite the noise: VIOLET searches the sky, JADE paints furiously, FUCHSIA paces and smokes, GRAY lies in a drunken stupor on his desk. JERRY's red darkroom light comes up on him, dancing and developing as before. The projected photographs are again of the other four, but this time as small children. The lights fade to black, then the projections; music continues for a moment then stops abruptly; lights up sharply on the next night:*]

ACT 3

[*Lights up on JADE's cubicle. She is on the floor in a posture of exhaustion and defeat. On the easel is a large painting of an empty dog collar floating on a sky-blue background with rays of golden light shooting out from it, suggesting a religious icon. JADE gets to her knees before the painting.*]

JADE: Forgive me, Blini. I was wrong to fight you. I was wrong to struggle. Struggle is useless, I see that now. This is something much, much bigger than a dog portrait. Bigger than my cash commission. Even bigger than art. This has to do with some kind of, uh, mystical transcendent zeitgeist kind of thing. I don't know; this isn't my usual gig. But it's clear that I have been...chosen to, uh, herald the arrival of, um, something. A new religion? The Cult of the Poodle? The Sacrament of the Divine Poodle? Blini, Poodle of God? Maybe we should leave the poodle part out. That could be for, like, initiates. The final, inner-most secret, the highest wisdom. "God is a light-gray miniature poodle named Blini." Yeah, that could work. Meanwhile, what should I do? Go door to door and spread the word? Ooh, I don't think so. Everybody hates those proselytizing creeps. I don't think I could do that. So, uh, what, get a P.A. system and stand on a street corner? Shave my head poodle-style and dance in front of pet stores? Come on, speak to me. Speak! [*Barking:*] Ruff! Ru-ru-ru-ru-ruff! [*Revelation:*] Ohh. Of course. Of course. I've been chasing my tail here. And the answer's right in front of me. I've got to keep painting. That's how You speak. Through me, through my brush, onto the canvas. I am the conduit, the path, the channel. Yeah. I have been touched by the Paw of Dog. I must paint. My art will show the way.

[*Lights cross to* GRAY, *euphoric, with bottle of Stolichnaya; during the following he may occasionally sing the text in the style of a Russian folk song.*]

GRAY: Ya chusvuyu namnoga luchey.Yuminya vasneeckla chuvsva zaquonchinetsi, yasnayu k'toh ya! *Ya Gray!* Hey! Ya Gray! Oh, yatak shesliv! Shtoza obligchenya! Tolka f'cheera ya chuvstvaval shtomaya zheezn koenchinah, shtouminya nyet budushiva, evdruck, vcyo ismenylos! Shto yeshi ya cirota? Nyeh vashno! Zheezen prekrazna! Ya nyamagu dazshdatsa uveditz me studentuf snova. Ya chuvstruya vdruck shto nam yestch shto skazatch druck drugh. Nashi rasgarory beeli tak ograneechenee, tak skuchnee. K'chorto! Me vseer brachea y sostri. Me dukshnee deleetza druck drugan. Y, oh, eta Galina. Moshit beet tiper. Ya smaya uhazshevat zanyey ana takaya interestnaya. Da! Da! Da! Da! Da!

(I feel so much better. I am feeling a sense of completeness, of being whole again, of knowing who I am! *I am Gray!* Hey! I am Gray! Oh, I am so happy! What a relief! Only yesterday I was feeling so miserable, as if my life was over, as if I had no future, and now, so quickly, everything has changed! So what if I'm an orphan? I don't care! Life is beautiful! I can't wait to see my students again. I feel suddenly that we have so much to say to each other. Our conversations have been so limited, so boring, so repetitive. To hell with that! We are all brothers and sisters. We must bare our souls to each other. And, oh, that Galina. Maybe now I could ask her out. She's so, I don't know, so interesting. Yes! Yes! Yes! Yes! Yes!)

[*Lights up on* VIOLET.]

VIOLET: Flock? Flock? Ohh, this is terrible. How did this happen? How could I let this happen? How could I lose my flock? Didn't they even notice? Will they come back for me? No, no, they can't, they have to keep going, they can't turn back. Oh, no. Oh, no. Should I try to catch up? I could, I could try, I know my vector, I know which way is south. But, but, but, but, but I, but I'm, but what if I get lost, what if I can't catch up, what if I'm flying out over the ocean and get tired and lose altitude and fall and fall and fall into the sea and sink and sink and sink until I drown?...Flock? Flock?

[*Lights up on* GRAY, *shouting down-stage out his window:*]

GRAY: Kamu nuzchen Angleeski? Uminya Ruskaya dushah! Oh, zheezen prekrazna! (Who needs English? I have a Russian soul! Oh, life is beautiful!)

VIOLET: [*Hearing* GRAY; *leaning out of window.*] Flock? Flock! [*Sees* GRAY; *startled scream:*] Aah!

GRAY: AAAH! Borgia! Ti eespogal minya! (Jesus! You scared me!)

VIOLET: What?!

GRAY: Shto? [*She starts to go.*] Padashdi! (What? Wait!)

VIOLET: What do you want?!

GRAY: K'toh tee? Shtoa tee hochish? (Who are you? What do you want?)

VIOLET: What? I can't understand you! I'm sorry—I thought I heard my flock. [*A little slower and louder:*] My. Flock. [*Normally:*] But, but they're not—

GRAY: Tee Stiya? (Your flock?)

VIOLET: [*Overlapping*]—not here, you're not—Look, I'm sorry—

GRAY: Padashdi! (Wait!)

[*The lights up on* FUCHSIA.]

FUCHSIA: Deserine lay in the shadow of a boulder. Soon the sun would rise higher and rob her of even this meager refuge. She had finished her last sip of bottled water. The last of the sun block had been used up the day before. Already the sand was hot. She watched the heat shimmering up off it. It was an effect she'd seen before, in the movies maybe, or in car commercials. It was prettier live. So was she, she couldn't help thinking. It had been days since she'd eaten anything. For the first time in her life she kind of wished she'd allowed herself a little more body fat. In case of emergencies. But she felt sure her story wasn't over yet. "After all," she thought in the far-off part of her brain that was still thinking, "I'm Deserine duPrey! I am absolutely guaranteed a happy ending." Suddenly she heard a voice.

VIOLET: "Ah, but that was before you rejected the formula."

FUCHSIA: Deserine focused her eyes with a tremendous effort. Directly in front of her, standing on one foot on the sand, was a bird. It appeared to be some kind of migratory sea bird. This seemed unlikely. Maybe she was hallucinating. But what the hell. "Yes, that's true. But I don't care. I have no regrets. Even if I die here in this desert. I regret nothing!" The bird shrugged. A kind of bird shrug. I mean, birds don't have shoulders, but it managed a kind of birdy equivalent.

VIOLET: "Yeah, whatever. Listen, a little ways past that rock formation there's a desert spa resort. Pull yourself together, you can be there in time for water aerobics."

FUCHSIA: "Oh! But, why? If I'm not entitled to a happy ending anymore." The bird began to open its wings.

VIOLET: "Don't be so self-centered, they didn't put it there for you. 'Scuse me, gotta migrate."

FUCHSIA: The bird took off, and Deserine began to crawl again. "I could really go for a mud wrap," she mused. But an hour later, she was only halfway to the rock formation, and her strength was gone. She lay face down on the sand and felt the sun pounding her, flattening her out, baking her into a tortilla. She thought about a frozen margarita, no salt. Pale, limey green. Beads of condensation on the frosty glass. She'd lost all sense of time. Maybe she'd been lying here for hours. Maybe she was already dead. Maybe the voice she now heard was another hallucination.

GRAY: "Hey. Hochish veepeet?" ("Want a drink?")

FUCHSIA: Deserine cracked open her crusty eyelids and saw a wavery figure of a man. He was offering her a bottle. It looked like some kind of liquor bottle. She shook her head weakly. The man tipped the bottle and poured the clear liquid over Deserine's face. It was water. She reached out, took the bottle and drank deeply.

GRAY: "Harasho. Da?" ("Good. Yes?")

FUCHSIA: Deserine squinted at the man. He appeared to be some kind of a hermit, or pilgrim. He looked complicated and interesting. Deserine felt her heart lurch. Was this love? Or dehydration? "What language are you speaking?"

GRAY: "Nyeh sprashee vi." ("Don't ask.")

FUCHSIA: "And yet somehow I can understand you. Do you believe in love?"

GRAY: "Da, da. Knezshna. K'stati ya v'por eskya." ("Yes, yes. Of course. In fact, I'm on this quest.")

FUCHSIA: "A quest?"

GRAY: "Da, ya eshu etu p'teetsu. Tee neyah veedela yeeyo?" ("Yes, I'm looking for this bird. Have you seen her?")

FUCHSIA: A bird? Uh... well, yes. I, I did see a bird. She, um, I guess she flew that way.

GRAY: "Spaseeba." ("Thanks.")

FUCHSIA: Deserine watched him waver away through the heat rays, and, refreshed and inspired, began to crawl again. "Des duPrey," she reflected, "your life's a real page-turner!" Giggling weakly, she crawled into the shade of the big weird rock formation. To her surprise, there was someone else there. A woman, painting onto the side of the rock.

Deserine was seized by a strange and powerful feeling, a feeling that her adventures were just beginning.

[*Lights up on* JADE. *The canvas on the easel is blank and white. She is talking to* JERRY.]

JADE: I was abandoned in a museum and raised by kindly museum guards. So you see I'm pretty much at home with art. We used to make the rounds at night and I'd look at the art by flashlight. I have a fierce grasp of detail. It's the bigger picture I have trouble with. My earliest art memories are of the bottoms of paintings, the lower edges. Because I was little, you know. I didn't understand what the signatures were for a long time. I couldn't read yet. I thought they were art too. I didn't quite get that people make art. I think I thought art was a natural phenomenon. Like I thought that the statues of gods in the classical wing were petrified people, people who were under a witch's spell or something. There was one I had a wicked crush on. One of those beautiful young curly-haired athletes, lean marble body, sad empty eyes staring into the distance. Once at night I snuck out by myself with a flashlight, and climbed up onto his plinth, twining my tiny limbs around him, under the influence of some idiotic fairy tale. I kissed his cold, cold lips. No magical transformation. [*Slight pause.*] Life is so fucking disappointing. [*Slight pause.*] I don't know why I'm even talking to you. What does a photographer know about anything? Running around plagiarizing life and calling it art. Aaagh. Don't mind me. I'm just in a nasty funk 'cause I've been abandoned by my god. There's no reason for it, is there? You can see this paint brush in my hand, can't you? But there's the blank canvas. Blini has stopped speaking to me. Why? Why? I don't know. I don't know anything anymore. I surrendered to the will of god or something and now it's left me twisting in the wind. I look at this object in my hand and it's a stranger to me. I can't use it and it's stopped using me. It's 3 A.M.; do you know where your raison d'etre is? Yeah, yeah, yeah. What it boils down to, je suis fucked.

[*The music from* Rescue the Android *comes up very loud. Lights fade to black on the cubicles. Projections show photographs of a poodle, a southwestern desert, Russian architecture and a flock of birds. In the red light of his dark-room,* JERRY *puts photographs into a suitcase. Projections disappear and the music stops abruptly. Lights up simultaneously on the next night:*]

ACT 4

FUCHSIA: Deserine lost all interest in reaching the spa resort. She really wished she could stay in this moment forever, lying on the rough sand in a spot of relative coolness, with the pale blue sky above, and the faint scritching sound of the paint brush against the rock. Perhaps an hour passed in this way. Then the artist put down her brush. She picked up a canteen, drank from it, then came over to Deserine, hunkered down and offered it to her. Deserine drank. "Thank you." Deserine felt suddenly confused, even disoriented.

JADE: "What are you doing out here in the desert?"

FUCHSIA: "I'm, well, I guess I'm on a quest. Yes. That's right. A quest."

JADE: "A quest for what?"

FUCHSIA: "For, for romance. What's funny?"

JADE: "Romance isn't a destination. It's a window into the infinite. A glimpse of the transcendent. A crack in the wall of cruel logic that we call reality, our one fragile link with the heavenly spheres...What's funny?"

FUCHSIA: "I don't know... Can I look at what you've been painting?"

JADE: "Sure."

FUCHSIA: Deserine got to her feet. She walked a few steps. She looked at the painting. The world tilted, spun, and shuddered. She staggered back. She looked at the woman.

JADE: "Cool, huh."

[*Lights cross to* JADE. *The canvas is still blank.*]

JADE: I wonder how long this could last. Will they find me here in 60 years covered in cobwebs, my paints dried to dust, clutching a paint brush in one wizened claw? Or will I hang myself tomorrow with tied-together strips of canvas? Or maybe in a couple of months I'll wash my hands, comb my hair, go out and get a real job. Lots of people do that. Get a real job with benefits and shit. Open a bank account. Buy

some furniture at Ikea. Walk half a mile out of my way to avoid passing a museum the rest of my life. [*Slight pause.*] Help.

[*Lights cross back to* VIOLET, *now hunched under her desk.*]

VIOLET: It's getting colder. It's colder every day. Soon it will be winter.
And what will I do? Without a flock. It will be a long, cold winter, without a flock. Very long. Long and cold. The snow will drift up. The
wind will bite through my feathers. I won't be able to find food, there
will be no food, no body warmth, no warm bird bodies around me,
the flock will come back in the spring and all they'll find will be my
lifeless cold frozen little dried-up skeletal skinny dead old carcass.

[GRAY *appears in her cell.*]

GRAY: Minya nuzshna pogovoreet stoboi. (I have to talk to you.)

VIOLET: Aah! What?

GRAY: Pajalista nyeh boysia, ya toilka hachu pogovoreet stoboi! (Please
don't be afraid, I just want to talk to you!)

VIOLET: What? I don't understand you!

GRAY: Ya znayu! Borgia! Minya nuzshnu shtobey tee ponila! (I know! God!
I have to make you understand!)

VIOLET: What?

GRAY: F'so beloh harasho, ya dumul shtoya sheshliv, y vdruck ya uveedel
teebeh! (Everything was fine, I thought I was happy and then I saw
you!)

VIOLET: I'm sorry, I—

GRAY: Ya uveedel teebeh! (I saw you!)

VIOLET: I can't understand you!

GRAY: *Aaagh!!*

[*Lights cross-fade to* FUCHSIA.]

FUCHSIA: Deserine lay on her back and looked up at the stars. They seemed unusually sharp and clear. It seemed to her that she could see them moving, very slowly moving in a vast and gorgeous pattern. The artist put another log on the little open fire, came back and lay down next to her again. Deserine slipped her arm around her shoulders and pulled her close. Her hair smelled like wood smoke. Somewhere in the distance a coyote yapped.

[*Pause. She has no idea what's next.* JADE *enters* FUCHSIA's *room suddenly, speaking without a pause:*]

JADE: Look you don't know me I have the studio next door and I know you'll think I'm crazy or disturbed or some kind of mentally ill and maybe I am maybe I am but please I don't know you but I'll listen to anyone I have a feeling a single word will make everything fall into place a single world will make everything make sense the right word will illuminate me entirely and I'll be able to affect my life again I'll be able to work again my hands will once again receive instructions from that place in my brain where the good stuff comes from the stuff you can't choose the stuff that chooses you who is this talking I can't recognise my own voice you wouldn't know about that you don't know me but you're a person you're another human person in the world and I trust you implicitly or explicitly I trust you and I know you can help me I know you know I know you can tell me where the art is.

FUCHSIA: Oh!

JADE: What?

FUCHSIA: Art isn't a destination. It's a window into the infinite. [*Slight pause.*] Maybe.

JADE: Oh. [*Slight pause.*] Same boat, huh?

[*Lights up on* VIOLET's *cell.*]

VIOLET: I used to dream about Star Trek all the time. The original series. And I would have my own bridge station over next to Scotty's, you know, across from Mr. Spock's, and it wasn't the most crucial or the most important station but I had my job to do and I knew what to do and I was good at it, and we all had our stations and we all knew what to do. And over and over we saved a world or even the universe, and then we'd all have a little laugh together, and on we'd go.

GRAY: Ya znayu tochnah achum tee gavaresh. (I know exactly what you're talking about.)

VIOLET: I can tell you know what I'm talking about. I wish I could understand you. I feel sure I would know just what to say, if I knew what you were talking about.

GRAY: Nyet, no ya magu tibya pomoch, ya pokazchu tibyeh shtoya tvoa staia, eli ya hachu beet yayu. (No, but, I could help you, I could show you that I'm your flock, or I want to be.)

VIOLET: [*Having listened hard.*] ... No. I just can't get it.

[*They look at each other. Lights up on* FUCHSIA's *cell. Rapidly and rhapsodically:*]

FUCHSIA: I don't know if I can do what I do anymore.

JADE: Me too.

FUCHSIA: I don't know where to go from here.

JADE: Me neither.

FUCHSIA: I'm blank, I'm bemused—

JADE: Yes—

FUCHSIA: I sense possibilities.

JADE: Yes—

FUCHSIA: I'm overwhelmed with possibilites.

JADE: I know.

FUCHSIA: I'm becalmed, adrift.

JADE: The horse latitudes, yes.

FUCHSIA: But there's a current.

JADE: But is there?

FUCHSIA: Yes, there are possibilities but I don't know.

JADE: What—

FUCHSIA: Or where—

JADE: Or how—

FUCHSIA: Yes or how—

JADE: Me too, I just don't *know.

FUCHSIA: [*Overlapping.*] Know, I just don't *know.

JADE: [*Overlapping.*] Know, I just don't *know.

FUCHSIA: [*Overlapping.*] *Know, I *just don't—

JADE: [*Overlapping.*] Just don't—

[*Slight pause.*]

FUCHSIA: Have you ever had the feeling that there's something else, besides everything you can think of, that everything you can think of isn't everything there is?

JADE: You mean besides money, and art—

FUCHSIA: And sex—

JADE: Work—

FUCHSIA: Spirituality—

JADE: Pleasure—

FUCHSIA: Survival.

JADE: Is that everything?

FUCHSIA: I think those are the catagories, those contain everything else.

JADE: Fashion?

FUCHSIA: Pleasure.

JADE: Science?

FUCHSIA: Survival. See, it's everything I can think of but I feel—

JADE: There's something else?

FUCHSIA: Something unnameable?

[*Pause. Lights up on* VIOLET'*s cell. She is indicating each thing she names, speaking slowly and clearly. She pauses slightly after each word, giving* GRAY *a chance to repeat it. He does not try to speak.*]

VIOLET: Pencil. Telephone. Table. Chair. Light. Window. Hand. Arm. Shoulder. Neck. Chin. Mouth. Mouth. [VIOLET *and* GRAY *kiss.*] Kiss.

FUCHSIA: OK, this is what I think.

JADE: OK.

FUCHSIA: It's the dark before the dawn.

JADE: Well, yeah.

FUCHSIA: No, I mean, figuratively. Metaphorically.

JADE: Oh.

FUCHSIA: I mean. I mean, it's 4 A.M. on Avenue B and the sun will come up and the sun will go down and sooner or later everything will be different.

VIOLET: It's all right. You don't have to talk.

GRAY: My name is Gray. What is your name?

[*Music up loud.* JERRY *dances downstage with suitcase, takes picture of the audience, exits.*]

END OF PLAY

I WILL GO... I WILL GO...

Glen Berger

I Will Go... I Will Go... by Glen Berger. Copyright © 1996 by Glen Berger. All rights reserved. Reprinted by permission of the author.

CAUTION: Professionals and amateurs are hereby warned that *I Will Go... I Will Go...* by Glen Berger is subject to a royalty. It is fully protected under the copyright laws of the United States of America, and of all countries covered by the International Copyright Union (including the Dominion of Canada and the rest of the British Commonwealth), and of all countries covered by the Pan-American Copyright Convention and the Universal Copyright Convention, and of all countries with which the United States has reciprocal copyright relations. All rights, including professional, amateur, motion picture, recitation, lecturing, public reading, radio broadcasting, television, video or sound taping, all other forms of mechanical or electronic reproduction, such as information storage and retrieval systems and photo-copyright, and the rights of translation into foreign languages are strictly reserved. Particular emphasis is laid upon the question of readings, permission for which must be secured from the author's agent in writing.

All inquiries concerning performance rights should be addressed to Joyce Ketay, Joyce Ketay Agency, 1501 Broadway, Suite 1908, New York, N.Y. 10036.

Glen Berger

GLEN BERGER was head writer for the Mask and Wig Comedy Troupe at the University of Pennsylvania before relocating to Seattle, where he was a member of Annex Theatre. He has spent the last six-plus years in New York with his wife. His plays include *Underneath the Lintel* (2001 L.A. Ovation Award for Best Play), *Great Men of Science*, Nos. 21 & 22 (1998 Ovation Award and 1998 L.A. Weekly Award for Best Play), *The Wooden Breeks, Bessemer's Spectacles* (1993 King County Emerging Artist's Grant), and *The Birdwatcher* (Seattle, First Place in 1990 New City Playwrights Festival). Glen was a recipient of a Manhattan Theatre Club Sloan Foundation commission, is a recent inductee to New Dramatists, and is a member of MCC Theater's Writers Coalition.

CHARACTERS:

H.F. SULLIVAN
STANLEY MERKEL, his trainer
GRACE, his ex-love
CHARLES HARRIS, Grace's new love
NARRATOR OMNISCIENT
CHORUS #1-4
PASSENGER #1
PASSENGER #2
REPORTER #1
REPORTER #2
SULLIVAN PROXY

NOTES:

SULLIVAN is preferably a largish man. Fat even.
SULLIVAN is painfully earnest, the REPORTER is earnest, MERKEL, the trainer, is earnest, they are all earnest.
During SULLIVAN'S flashbacks with GRACE, a "SULLIVAN PROXY" should take over the swimming chores for SULLIVAN. Dressed in identical bathing costume.

[*In darkness we hear a musical montage of vintage recordings of WWI songs, overlapping each other to eerie effect, combined with sounds of bombs exploding, machine gun fire, troops marching, etc. This transmutes into solemn and beautiful music as—*]

NARRATOR OMNISCIENT: This earth…this solemn earth… turns … this 4 A.M.… 1923… turns while the ex-German soldier adjusts his prosthesis in his sleep, and behind a couch in a living room, a spider struggles to free itself from a ball of lint—

CHORUS #1: The living slumber—

CHORUS #2: The dead molder—

CHORUS #3: Dogs bark—

CHORUS #4: Stars twinkle…

NARRATOR OMNISCIENT: And on a beach... in the pale dark before dawn, stands H.F. Sullivan, one man, alone, in bathing costume, slathered in lubricant. What thoughts... what thoughts thought by this man, on this Dover beach, this near-dawn night...

SULLIVAN: I will go... I will go... I will put this beach behind me... I will put it all behind me... France lies beyond... I will employ the Trudgen stroke... A breeze, from the northeast—the channel will be cold... but no matter... no matter...

NARRATOR OMNISCIENT: A surgeon takes off his gloves, there was nothing he could do, a spider struggles in its ball of lint, and on a beach in Dover, one man, in bathing costume—

MERKEL: And joining him, his trainer...

REPORTER #1: ... and reporters...

[*Beat.*]

Many have tried, many have failed...

SULLIVAN: Yes.

REPORTER #1: Matthew Webb was the first to swim the Channel, in 1879...

MERKEL: He was. He crossed it in 21 hours and some change.

REPORTER #1: And T.W. Burgess did it in 1911...

MERKEL: Yes, again in 21 hours, but our man Sullivan is the first American who will accomplish it. And he will do it in the record time of 16 hours. He will be in France in time for a late supper.

REPORTER #1: And what will you do for nourishment in the hard hours til then?

SULLIVAN: I will utilize a feed mechanism that I've developed with Stanley Merkel my trainer...

REPORTER #1: How does it work?

MERKEL: I'll be in the boat nearby. On the hour, food will be passed to him via this tube. What has been the undoing of so many will not be the undoing of Sullivan.

REPORTER #1: But why Mr. Sullivan... why are you doing this... Putting your life and health on the line?

SULLIVAN: There has been talk that this world makes little sense... that there's little worth in making an effort... but...

[*His voice begins to crack.*]

... but all the horrors we have seen in our lifetimes... all that we've endured, we must understand that it was not in vain... and that with perseverance, we can forge ahead, put... all that... behind us, and know that we are better men for what we have endured... And the thought that perhaps, should I make it, even at the end of the century they'll remember me... in moments of darkness... to help them go on... That is enough...

NARRATOR OMNISCIENT: On a beach in Dover, a reporter who never learned shorthand hurriedly writes down what he has just heard... On this almost-dawn night, the sound of surf... and the scratch of a pencil... and nothing else...

REPORTER #1: [*Writing.*] ... in vain... perseverance... endure... darkness...

[*The scrawling continues. Then, finally:*]

But one last question... Mr. Sullivan... In all your days of endurance swimming... the records set... and now this, the Channel... twenty-one miles of it... good god... twenty-one miles.... what is the secret?

SULLIVAN: Secret?

REPORTER #1: What keeps you going, when all seems bleak and black and hopeless?

SULLIVAN: I sing songs to myself.

REPORTER #1: Songs? Any favorites?

SULLIVAN: There's plenty I love, and cherish, but none more than the songs of Henry Burr… 700 tunes recorded and all of them… lovely…

REPORTER #1: All the world knows Burr—

SULLIVAN: Burr, he's the one for when you're halfway cross the sea….

[*And we hear softly a Burr recording of something gentle, e.g. "What Does it Matter."*]

… I imagine that golden tenor streaming out of the gramophone and all the chill of the channel, and all the rest of my troubles, fade… Henry Burr—there's a name that will live on in the hearts of men.

REPORTER #1: Just like H.F. Sullivan, eh? "First American to swim the Channel!"

SULLIVAN: Please understand. I am just a man… But I will go… I will see you in 16 hours, in France!

NARRATOR OMNISCIENT: A photograph is taken.

[*We hear the sound of waves, gulls, etc.*]

The earth turns from west to east, in Cork the first rumble of trucks and trams, a spider behind a couch struggles in a ball of lint, millions are in offices—

CHORUS #1: In beds—

CHORUS #2: In fields—

CHORUS #3: In kitchens—

CHORUS #4: In factories—

NARRATOR OMNISCIENT: But one man in all the world is in a bathing costume in the English Channel, slathered in lubricant.

[*We see* SULLIVAN *in midst of swim* [*supine on a table*] *(and he continues swimming unless otherwise noted), we hear him breathing... and then:*]

MERKEL: [*To self, standing in a representation of a boat, perhaps with megaphone.*] That's it... Left... right... left... Yes, the Trudgen stroke —like the Australian crawl, it involves alternate overarm strokes from a prone position, but a scissors kick is used, and the head remains on one side... How do you do it? The water today is 48 degrees Fahrenheit. I can teach you the strokes... but the Will... the Will... that is something else altogether...

SULLIVAN: [*To self.*] Is it still before dawn?... Where is the sun?... Will morning never come?... Perhaps morning will never come...

NARRATOR OMNISCIENT: And then... just then... to his left... to his east... against the odds... the sun...

[*We see the sun, made rather ineptly out of construction paper, rise slowly, accompanied by achingly beautiful music, e.g. the opening of the third movement of Beethoven's* String Quartet, op. 135.]

SULLIVAN: I've never seen anything more beautiful...

MERKEL: [*Calling out.*] Are you all right?

SULLIVAN: Fine!... all will be fine...

[*We hear Burr's "What Does it Matter" and a flashback ensues: lights up on a box of flowers just opened... and then a phone... and then a woman on the phone, smiling, almost giddily, at flowers...*]

GRACE: Windsor 8-2000 please.

[*A phone rings. The* "SULLIVAN PROXY" *takes over swimming duties from* SULLIVAN *in a formal exchange.* SULLIVAN *sits down at small desk and answers the phone.*]

SULLIVAN: Hello?

[*There is a great amount of static over the telephone line. Still they struggle on with the conversation...*]

GRACE: [*Referring to flowers.*] They're beautiful.

SULLIVAN: So you got them?

GRACE: I can barely hear you.

SULLIVAN: What?

GRACE: My love... Are you almost done?

SULLIVAN: What?

GRACE: Are you almost done?!

SULLIVAN: I still have paperwork...

GRACE: What?

SULLIVAN: Are you smiling?

GRACE: When are you coming home?

SULLIVAN: Are you sure that's what you want?

GRACE: What?

SULLIVAN: Do you really want me home?

GRACE: Yes.

SULLIVAN: What?...

GRACE: Can you hear me?

SULLIVAN: [*Speaking softly and slowly, with grin, completely to self.*] Through the static... I can hear your smile... I can hear your love... Yes... I can hear you fine...

[*Song continues, lights down on* SULLIVAN *at desk... Song cuts off abruptly, to sound of waves,* SULLIVAN *takes over swimming from* PROXY, *and we see him struggling in the water.*]

NARRATOR OMNISCIENT: Bilge. Bilge from ships, slicks of oil, and sewage from coastal towns can abound and be encountered by a swimmer attempting a Channel crossing. And these are just some of the difficulties in a cross-channel swim. Great schools of jellyfish are another.

MERKEL: Are you all right? Sullivan? Call an end to it Sullivan! There's swarms of jellyfish. They'll do you in!

NARRATOR OMNISCIENT: The poisonous nettles will nestle inside the bathing costume of H.F. Sullivan. They will remain for the duration. Darts and stabbings of horrible pain, the extremities of Sullivan inflamed... throbbing... and yet...

SULLIVAN: I will not come out... I will go on...

[*And we hear "What Does it Matter" by Burr, and in a flashback: we see* SULLIVAN *and* GRACE *(*SULLIVAN PROXY *having taken over swimming duty). It is clear that* GRACE *is sadly aware of the tragedy that is about to befall* SULLIVAN—*she is about to cut him loose.*]

SULLIVAN: My love... my dear Grace... You in my arms...

GRACE: Yes.

SULLIVAN: How right it feels... how right... I never want to leave this...

GRACE: Look I...

SULLIVAN: What is it?

GRACE: ... Your hair... is still wet... You'll catch your death...

SULLIVAN: No... the day's training is done and now I'm home... and the fireplace, this room, and this love will keep me warm... but is that a tear my darling?

GRACE: No....

NARRATOR OMNISCIENT: And above the hearth was carved this: "Two lovebirds built this nest..."

SULLIVAN: I'm close... a year at the most before the day, that day, the channel swim... that dream we share...

GRACE: Know this, H.F. Sullivan—that I will always believe in your ability...

SULLIVAN: I do know... And know this my Only... that my swim I will have dedicated to you, and you alone, for it was your faith that—

GRACE: [*Interrupting him.*] Yes but...

[*She cries.*]

... Look... look I...

SULLIVAN: Yes?

GRACE : There's... someone else.

SULLIVAN: What?... What do you mean?

GRACE: There's someone else. And I love him. And that's... that's it really... There's someone else.

[*We hear only Burr on the gramophone.*]

SULLIVAN: [*Devastated.*] Who? Who is he?

GRACE: You don't know him.... I had to tell you...

SULLIVAN: What's his name?

GRACE: It doesn't matter, you don't know him...

SULLIVAN: How could this happen? What went wrong?

GRACE: I'm sorry, I—

SULLIVAN: Was there something I could have changed? What did you say his name was?

GRACE: You don't know him.

SULLIVAN: But what is it?

GRACE: What does it matter? You don't know him.

SULLIVAN: Tell me his name! At least give me that!

GRACE: But you've never heard of him!

SULLIVAN: I want to know his name!

GRACE: Charles Harris!

SULLIVAN: Charles Harris?

   [*Pause.*]

   Who's Charles Harris?

GRACE: You don't know him.

   [*Pause.*]

   But he's the man I love.

SULLIVAN: Grace... but my god... How can you say that?

GRACE: I'm sorry. But it's the truth...

SULLIVAN: And yet... we are here, embracing...

GRACE: And yet—

SULLIVAN: All is lost, isn't it... and we are not embracing...

GRACE: No... We separated long ago...

SULLIVAN: And you... where are you now...? In a cottage for two? By the fire? With a song on the gramophone?

GRACE: And you? Where are you?

SULLIVAN: I?... am in the English Channel...

[*We hear the blast of a ship's horn, which brings* SULLIVAN *out of his reverie. Music fades, and lights slowly up on* SULLIVAN, *who has traded positions with the* PROXY *and is swimming again.*]

Put it behind you... put it behind you... The Trudgen stroke will carry us through...

MERKEL: Sullivan! Can you hear me! You must come out! It's begun to rain and the boat is leaking water. We have to turn back!

SULLIVAN: Turn back then. I will go on...

MERKEL: Sullivan! The tides are carrying us miles off course! We won't make it in 16 hours... I'm losing sight of you! Another time, another day—we'll try again! Sullivan, can you hear me!

NARRATOR OMNISCIENT: No, he cannot hear you... He has lost sight of the boat... This one man, alone, no longer slathered in lubricant, the chafing wind, the chafing water, has swept and washed most of the lubricant away and now chill has worked its way into the flesh and marrow of this one man... To his right, to the west, the pale sun sets...

SULLIVAN: And will the sun rise again? Yes... the sun will rise again... but will I see it?

[*There is now complete and utter darkness on stage.*]

NARRATOR OMNISCIENT: In the darkness he swims. In total darkness he swims, though we cannot see it. And yet, we will watch...

SULLIVAN: [*In darkness.*] To hell with posterity... to hell with this... perseverance be damned, it's all blather and I'll have drowned for nothing... And even if it isn't for nothing that I'll have drowned, even if it turns out that I'll have drowned for something, the truth will still be this: that I'll have drowned.

NARRATOR OMNISCIENT: But just then... to his left, to the east... the pale moon rises.

[*Lights fade up as inept moon of construction paper rises to same beautiful music as before.*]

SULLIVAN: Yes, the moon! Of course! The moon will guide me.... You will not drift... The Trudgen stroke will see you through... and if not that... then another... there's no turning back... I will go on...

[*We hear Burr's "What Does it Matter" as* SULLIVAN *continues swimming.*]

NARRATOR OMNISCIENT: And three moths flap and knock against the beaming bulb of a Novalux streetlamp in Milford, New Jersey... and one man, in the lobby of the Hotel Excelsior, in a phone booth...

CHARLES HARRIS: [*On phone.*] I was wrong... terribly wrong... But look, do you... Do you forgive me?

[*And lights up on* GRACE *on phone.*]

GRACE: Yes... I do... But do you, Charles Harris, forgive *me*?

[*Pause.*]

HARRIS: [*Tenderly.*] There's nothing to forgive.

GRACE: Where are you?

HARRIS: That doesn't matter now... I'm coming home... Leave a light in the window will you?

GRACE: Oh you can bet on it... but Charles—

HARRIS: Yes?

GRACE: Hurry.

HARRIS: I'm coming home...

NARRATOR OMNISCIENT: And buffeted by waves and wind, limbs numb, ears ringing, in the rain, in the dark, tides carrying him miles this way, then miles that—H.F. Sullivan. And dodging ships, that too he must contend with, in this busiest of shipping lanes—past cable ships for phone lines—

CHORUS #1: And dredging ships for dredging—

CHORUS #2: Mail steamers and oil tankers—

CHORUS #3: Buoy tenders—

CHORUS #4: And boats for shipping bananas.

[*Pause.*]

CHORUS #1: And melons.

NARRATOR OMNISCIENT: And not noticing the swimming man below them, on a luxury liner headed to America, two men discuss:

PASSENGER #1: My trousers. I sent my trousers with the steward to be pressed and he never returned with them.

PASSENGER #2: Which trousers are those?

PASSENGER #1: The grey serge.

PASSENGER #2: Ah. When I asked them to bring down a particular shaving soap I forgot to pack, they came in half a shake.

PASSENGER #1: Ha. Did they.

PASSENGER #2: Sensitive skin.

PASSENGER #1: What shaving soap then do you use?

PASSENGER #2: Whitney's No. 2.

PASSENGER #1: Ah, Whitney's… Lathers up nicely then?

PASSENGER #2: Like a charm. So look, if you need to borrow a pair of trousers—

PASSENGER #1: Oh thank you, I'll be fine… but it's nice to know someone cares.

PASSENGER #2: Well if I didn't care, you can take solace that at least there's the stars above taking note.

PASSENGER #1: My dear friend… there's nothing I'm more sure of than the cold ambivalence of the stars…

NARRATOR OMNISCIENT: There is saltwater covering 70% of this old earth… and there is saltwater in the lungs of H.F. Sullivan… And at a traffic light, in a motor car, of the Ford make, Charles Harris waits.

[*Lights up on* CHARLES HARRIS, *at wheel of a car. Driving gloves on.*]

CHARLES HARRIS: It's always inadvisable to motor along a tram track, for tramlines, especially if they're wet, are most "skid-provoking…"

[*Shudders.*]

… that was close back there… rainy night… I must be more careful… I do want to make it home… to you… The pale moon is rising… Will you still be there when I return?… Under the moon, is there meaning?… We must swim towards love, and that is all…

[*Still swimming.*]

SULLIVAN: I can't make it… not in the dark… not in this—no, Sullivan… say to yourself… morning will come… morning will come… it's darkest before the dawn…

NARRATOR OMNISCIENT: And then... just then... the pale sun against the odds... rises...

[*We see the same sun of construction paper rise to the same music.*]

Morning has come... 24 hours and more now Sullivan has been in that strait the French call La Manche, and the English call the English Channel...

SULLIVAN: But I'll make it now... I'll make it surely...

[*We see that* HARRIS *has returned home.* GRACE *puts down her book— a moment between the two, and they embrace...*]

And perhaps... and perhaps... she is thinking of me....

[*But she and* HARRIS *are in mute, passionate embrace.*]

Perhaps she is wondering where I am?... Perhaps yes!... Yes, I will go on... and France awaits... We must swim towards love... We must... That is all we can do...

NARRATOR OMNISCIENT: And all this lousy old earth turns... The ex-German soldier adjusts his prosthesis in his sleep, dogs bark, stars twinkle, and behind a couch a spider lies motionless and dead within the tangles of lint and dust... and the spider will be indistinguishable from the dust soon enough... And on the shore, in France, one man in bathing costume, his hearing impaired, permanently, from the icy waters...

REPORTER #2: You have done it Mr. Sullivan, you have done it... Carried by tides for an astonishing 53 miles, in the chill waters for 27 hours and 32 minutes, nevertheless you have crossed the Channel, and what is more, the first American to do so...

SULLIVAN: What? I can't hear you.

NARRATOR OMNISCIENT: In three years, Gertrude Ederle, the first woman to swim the Channel, will accomplish the task in 14 hours and 31 minutes.

REPORTER #2: You have done it, sir! You have crossed the Channel ... Such perseverance will go down in history... Your name will be remembered, all that misery is behind you now... You have done it... you have crossed the Channel. I'm sure this task accomplished is most meaningful to you, isn't it?... Most meaningful...

[*Pause.*]

SULLIVAN: Yes.

NARRATOR OMNISCIENT: Or perhaps he merely shrugs. Shrugs from not knowing the answer... or shrugs because he still cannot hear the question...

[*Up on music.*]

<u>END OF PLAY</u>

THE SIREN SONG OF STEPHEN JAY GOULD

Benjamin Bettenbender

The Siren Song of Stephen Jay Gould by Benjamin Bettenbender. Copyright ©
2002 by Benjamin Bettenbender. All rights reserved. Reprinted by permission
of the author.

CAUTION: Professionals and amateurs are hereby warned that *The Siren
Song of Stephen Jay Gould* by Benjamin Bettenbender is subject to a royalty. It is
fully protected under the copyright laws of the United States of America, and of
all countries covered by the International Copyright Union (including the
Dominion of Canada and the rest of the British Commonwealth), and of all
countries covered by the Pan-American Copyright Convention and the
Universal Copyright Convention, and of all countries with which the United
States has reciprocal copyright relations. All rights, including professional, amateur, motion picture, recitation, lecturing, public reading, radio broadcasting,
television, video or sound taping, all other forms of mechanical or electronic
reproduction, such as information storage and retrieval systems and photo-copyright, and the rights of translation into foreign languages are strictly reserved.
Particular emphasis is laid upon the question of readings, permission for which
must be secured from the author's agent in writing.

All inquiries concerning performance rights should be addressed to Bruce
Ostler, Brett Adams Agency, 448 West 44th Street, New York, N.Y. 10036.

Benjamin Bettenbender

BENJAMIN BETTENBENDER is the author of *Vick's Boy* (Circa Theatre, American Theater Company, Rattlestick Productions), *Scaring the Fish* (in New York at the INTAR and in San Francisco at the Magic Theatre), *Those Left Behind* (The Directors Company), *Bliss* (Currican), *Widow's Walk* (The Levin Theater Company, New Brunswick, New Jersey, and at the Summer NITE Festival in Chicago), *Emil* (The Levin Theater Company), and *A Second Wind* (Rutgers University, the Jan Hus Theater in New York, and The George Street Playhouse). He is a member of the Cape Cod Theatre Project, where four of his plays (*Scaring the Fish*, *Emil*, *Vick's Boy*, and *The Siren Song of Stephen Jay Gould*) have been performed.

CHARACTERS:

MAN
WOMAN

[*The bank of a river, near a bridge stanchion. A* WOMAN *walks slowly along the bank, staring across the water. She stops, lost in a moment. She then reaches into her pocket, removes something, hesitates, then pulls her arm back to throw. An anguished cry is heard from above that gets louder as it continues. She stops her throw and starts to look up when a* MAN *falls on her, knocking her over. The two roll down the bank, coming to rest in a twisted heap. Neither moves for a moment. Then the man slowly disengages himself and rolls away. He stands, placing his left foot down gingerly, wincing; he then looks back to her.*]

MAN: Oh my God.

[*He moves to her side, touching her lightly on the arm.*]

Are you all right? Miss?

[*She stirs but doesn't respond.*]

Miss, are you all right?

[*Shaking her a bit.*]

Miss, are you—

WOMAN: Oowwww!

MAN: Sorry. Sorry, sorry. I didn't know if—

WOMAN: What did you do?

MAN: Nothing. I just shook you.

WOMAN: Why?

MAN: To see if you were OK.

WOMAN: [*Trying to move her right arm.*] I think my arm is broke.

MAN: Oh God! Um... Move your fingers.

WOMAN: Why?

MAN: That's how you tell.

WOMAN: Tell?

MAN: If your arm is broke.

WOMAN: No it's not.

MAN: Yes it is.

WOMAN: That's how you tell if your fingers are broke.

MAN: No, 'cause they freeze up.

WOMAN: Excuse me?

MAN: Your fingers. When your arm is broke.

WOMAN: So how do you tell if your fingers are broke?

MAN: X-rays. Here, sit up.

> [*He tries to help her come to a full seated position, but she shrugs him off and does it herself. She removes the object she had been holding in her injured hand, gently prying it from her fingers, and places it back in her pocket. She then extends the arm out in front of her, staring at her stiff fingers.*]

Now try to move them.

WOMAN: I am.

MAN: Oh man, I knew it!

WOMAN: They're shaking a little.

MAN: Are you doing that on purpose?

WOMAN: No.

MAN: Bad sign.

WOMAN: In what way? Bad how?

MAN: It could be a fracture.

WOMAN: You already said it was broken.

MAN: Right, but a fracture is worse.

WOMAN: It's the same exact thing.

MAN: I don't think so. It's like another degree of break, with shards and stuff. That's why it sounds like that. *Frac*-ture. *Frac, frac.* See? Much worse than "break."

WOMAN: Shards?

MAN: Don't worry. It's fine as long as you don't get jostled.

WOMAN: What will that do?

MAN: You don't want to know.

WOMAN: You're bleeding.

MAN: I am?

WOMAN: Your head.

MAN: [*Dabbing at it.*] Is it bad?

WOMAN: I don't think so. It's just a little cut.

MAN: You're sure?

WOMAN: Yeah. At first I thought it was a laceration, but then I figured it was only a gash, but now I'm pretty sure it's—

MAN: Fine. Make fun, if you want.

[*He reaches into his pocket for a handkerchief, pressing it to the wound.*]

WOMAN: Can I ask you something?

MAN: What?

WOMAN: Well, I'm a little woozy still so I apologize if this sounds strange, but... did you jump on me? [*Pause. He doesn't answer.*] Did you?

MAN: Well, I wasn't... I didn't exactly, no.

WOMAN: Did you fall?

MAN: No.

WOMAN: Were you thrown?

MAN: I leapt.

WOMAN: I see.

[*Pause.*]

Then when you said no, what you really meant was yes, you *did* jump on me.

MAN: I guess so.

WOMAN: Were you trying to rob me?

MAN: No, I didn't even see you.

WOMAN: I was standing right here. Didn't you check first?

MAN: No. I was... I should have. It was irresponsible of me, but I thought I was over the water.

WOMAN: The water's way over there. It's low because of the drought.

MAN: I know. I mean, I realize that now.

WOMAN: And anyway, what were you doing...?

[*Pause.*]

Just a second.

MAN: Is it hurting?

WOMAN: No. I mean, yes, it is, but that's not the thing right now. It's just hard to express myself when I get this way.

MAN: Injured?

WOMAN: Angry.

MAN: Oh.

WOMAN: I mean, you... *jumped* on me!

MAN: And I'm really sorry.

WOMAN: How dare you?!

MAN: Really, *really* sorry.

WOMAN: You... idiot! You stupid idiot! You could have killed me.

MAN: I feel worse than I could ever tell you.

WOMAN: All because you couldn't bother to look before leaping off a bridge.

MAN: You know, maybe the thing to do right now would be to get you to a hospital in case—

WOMAN: And what kind of dunderhead goes swimming dressed like that? In jeans. And spats.

MAN: They're not spats.

WOMAN: Whatever. What sort of fool goes—

MAN: They're ankle weights.

WOMAN: Oh great. Even better. Why not strap a millstone around your neck while you're at it? That way you can be sure to...

[*She stops, stares at him.*]

Tell me this isn't what it looks like.

MAN: It is.

WOMAN: No way.

MAN: I'm serious.

WOMAN: Tell me you weren't trying... You weren't jumping...

MAN: To my death, yes.

[*Long pause. She then bursts out laughing.*]

Hey!

WOMAN: Off that little bridge.

[*She laughs harder.*]

With those things on your feet, without even checking to...

[*She laughs even more.*]

MAN: Excuse me?

WOMAN: The water...

[*Laughs.*]

MAN: What are you doing? What's so damn funny?

WOMAN: Even if you hit it, the water...

[*Laughs.*]

It would barely come up to your waist.

[*Laughs.*]

MAN: I told you I didn't know about—

WOMAN: You'd be standing there with your feet stuck in the mud with those ankle thingies on, trying to...

[*Laughing.*]

... trying to pull them out.

[*Mimes pulling a leg out of the mud.*]

Sssclorp!

[*Laughs uncontrollably.*]

MAN: All right, that's enough. I mean it. This isn't something you make fun of.

WOMAN: What, you mean trying to drown yourself in a puddle?

MAN: I didn't know it was this low, OK?

WOMAN: [*Suddenly serious.*] I was leaping into the mud... to my death.

[*Laughs.*]

MAN: I was trying to go head first, for your information, but the ankle weights swung me around when I was in the air so my feet came back under me and—

[*She laughs harder than ever.*]

That's it. I'm not talking to you.

[*He starts to limp off.*]

WOMAN: Wait, I'm sorry.

MAN: Forget it.

WOMAN: You're hurt.

MAN: Too damn bad.

WOMAN: Hey, stop, all right? I won't laugh anymore.

[*He has gone off.*]

And I could use some help myself! This was your fault, after all!

[*Pause.*]

You're not just going to leave me here, are you?!!!

[*Pause. He re-enters, limps over to her, holds out his hand to help her up.*]

In a minute. I'm still a little shaky.

MAN: From laughing.

WOMAN: From being landed on.

[*Pause.*]

So why were you jumping?

MAN: I told you.

WOMAN: Yeah, but why? Depressed?

MAN: What kind of question is that?

WOMAN: A logical question, I would think?

MAN: Right. And when you see a person lying down with their eyes closed, I suppose you ask if they're sleepy. Someone's chowing down on a plate of pasta, you wonder whether they're hungry. Duh.

WOMAN: Um... I hate to interrupt your mocking of me, but it's not really that simple. What you're talking about doing goes a little beyond basic bodily functions. It's not simple cause and effect.

MAN: Yes, I am depressed. Are you happy now? The answer to your question is yes.

WOMAN: Oh.

[*Pause.*]

Because you don't seem it.

MAN: Oh, that does it. I'm sitting over there.

WOMAN: Wait. I'm serious. Depression is a specific medical condition with a recognizable set of symptoms.

MAN: Well I have them. Plenty of them.

WOMAN: I don't see any.

MAN: That's because I'm irritated right now.

WOMAN: There you go. People in a suicidal depression don't get irritated like that. They're apathetic.

[*Pause.*]

MAN: [*Apathetic.*] Whatever.

WOMAN: That's why I thought it might be something else.

MAN: Like what?

WOMAN: An illness.

MAN: No.

WOMAN: Bad news. A loss.

MAN: No.

WOMAN: Fear.

MAN: Of what?

WOMAN: Someone's trying to kill you and you don't want to wait for it to happen so you do it yourself.

MAN: No.

WOMAN: Guilt.

MAN: Over what?

WOMAN: How should I know. Maybe you got into an argument and beat someone into a coma and found out later he was a Zen Buddhist who had taken a vow of nonviolence and couldn't defend himself, and he had six kids and was working on a cure for blindness.

MAN: What was the argument about?

WOMAN: Or maybe, *maybe*, it's love.

MAN: Love?

WOMAN: Maybe you're heartbroken over a romance that ended. Or that never was.

MAN: What's so bad about that?

WOMAN: Are you kidding? That's about the best reason of all to want to drown yourself. Meeting the person you want to be with forever, and then realizing it can never be. Knowing you'll grow old and die without ever again looking into the one set of eyes that brings peace to your heart. Someone who makes you feel like you can face anything in the world as long as you can do it squeezing their hand.

MAN: But you just said I didn't seem depressed.

WOMAN: That's not depression. That's something far more profound.

MAN: What, sulking?

WOMAN: What did you say?

MAN: Sulking. How is that more profound than depression?

WOMAN: I don't think you quite understand what I'm getting at.

MAN: What's not to understand? You like someone, they don't like you back. Woo-dee-woo-dee-woo. You mope around a few days, maybe a couple of weeks, play around with the idea of killing yourself just to show them how sorry they'll be when you're gone, then you get bored with it all, get interested in someone else, and fffffft! It's all better.

[*Pause. He sees her staring at him.*]

What?

[*Pause.*]

What is it? What?

WOMAN: I don't want to discuss this anymore.

MAN: But you brought it up.

WOMAN: That's before I realized you lacked the emotional sophistication to understand what true loss is. I should have guessed it, though, judging by your pathetic, halfhearted attempt to kill yourself.

MAN: Pathetic?! Half...! Listen, you judgmental... whatever, if we had gotten even half the rainfall we usually do, I'd be dead right now! Gone! Dragged to the bottom of a dark river with my lungs filled with water. And you'd have been on the shore watching the whole thing, thinking how depressed and emotionally sophisticated I was to have done it!

WOMAN: But you didn't, did you? And you want to know why you didn't? Because you're too shallow. Because you never experienced a pain so strong it would make eternal darkness seem like a bargain by comparison.

MAN: Oh, and you have, I suppose.

WOMAN: More than you, I can tell you that.

MAN: Then why are you here talking about it? Why aren't you floating around in eternal darkness all happy and carefree?

WOMAN: Listen, I was close. I was this close.

MAN: What, you gave your wrist a little scratch? Took a few too many aspirin?

WOMAN: I drank poison, bucko!

MAN: What kind?

WOMAN: None of your damn business!

MAN: Come on, you're so committed, tell me what kind of poison you drank. Maybe I'll go buy some.

[*Pause.*]

Well?

WOMAN: It was... I believed at the time... poison, and that's what matters.

MAN: What's that mean?

WOMAN: It means that even though what I drank—in the firm belief that I was, in fact, ending my life—even though it was still horrible and extremely dangerous in large doses, it wasn't... *technically*... poison.

MAN: So what was it? Buttermilk?

[*Pause.*]

WOMAN: Ipecac.

MAN: Pardon?

WOMAN: Ipecac. I drank ipecac.

[*Long pause.*]

MAN: But that's the stuff that makes you—

WOMAN: I know what it is *now*, all right?! I know better than anyone. But before that I had only been told never, ever to touch it, and my folks kept it on the top shelf of their medicine cabinet hidden in back, so I thought it must be lethal.

MAN: I bet it felt lethal.

WOMAN: You have no idea.

[*Pause. They sit a moment.*]

Anyway, I'm not going to make the same mistake again. As soon as I've completed a single, sweet, symbolic gesture, I'm going to go back and do it right.

MAN: What'll it be this time, death by Ex-lax?

[*She stares at him.*]

WOMAN: Why don't you just leave, all right?

MAN: What, you get to make fun of me, but I can't say the least little thing about you?

WOMAN: No, you got your dig in, you evened the score, so I don't see where we have anything else to discuss. Nice meeting you.

MAN: I thought you were hurt. You needed my help.

WOMAN: I'm better.

MAN: I thought your arm was broken.

WOMAN: It'll be fine.

MAN: Well I can't just leave you here.

WOMAN: Sure you can. Go back to playing in the mud. Goodbye.

[*He stands watching her a moment. He then takes a few limping steps away. He stops.*]

MAN: Hurt pretty bad, huh?

WOMAN: I told you not to worry about it.

MAN: No, the person. The ipecac guy. That must've been pretty awful for you to feel that way.

WOMAN: What, you mean "sulky"?

MAN: You know what I mean.

[*Pause.*]

WOMAN: It was pretty bad, yes.

[*Pause.*]

MAN: I'm sorry it happened to you.

WOMAN: Thank you.

[*They sit.*]

And I'm sorry that whatever happened to make you feel like jumping off a bridge happened to you.

[*Pause.*]

And if you don't tell me what it was, I'm going to strangle you with my good hand.

MAN: Hey, I don't know anything about you either.

WOMAN: You do too. You know I was in a romance that destroyed my will to live.

MAN: But you didn't go into any details.

WOMAN: After that "moping around" crack, you don't get details without earning them. So give, kamikaze. I'm laying odds on crushing gambling debts.

[*He doesn't answer at first.*]

MAN: Stephen Jay Gould.

WOMAN: Who?

MAN: He's this scientist up at Harvard.

WOMAN: And he flunked you and you had to drop out of school and it ruined your life. No wait, wait! He stole your research and published it and got famous and married your girlfriend, and you ended up broke and alone and bitter.

[*Pause. He stares at her.*]

Maybe you should just tell it.

MAN: He's an author. He writes about trilobites and dinosaurs and musicians, stuff like that. Anyway, a while back I got into a big argument with someone at work about why there are no .400 hitters anymore, and I—

WOMAN: You work at Harvard and you're arguing about baseball?

MAN: I don't work at Harvard. I work at a carpet warehouse. Anyway, I said it was relief pitching but he keeps going on about "the right wall of human physical achievement," and how I should read this book by this guy Gould.

WOMAN: About trilobites.

MAN: About evolution.

WOMAN: Not about baseball?

MAN: Yes about baseball. It's... complicated. He's writing about .400 hitters but he's really talking about how we're this big accident.

WOMAN: Us?

MAN: People. How most life on earth is basically bacteria, and how everything else is just sort of... *not* bacteria.

WOMAN: So?

MAN: Well the way he explained it made sense. I could see that it was all true, you know? I could see that life was pretty much just a lot of microbes swimming in the dirt, and all the things we see around us and find beautiful and live for are just... a fluke. They're this statistical aberration that could never be repeated if you started over. People, us, we would never happen again. There's nothing *inevitable* about any of it.

WOMAN: So what?

MAN: So everything. If we're just this oddball one-in-fifty million chance occurrence, then it means everything we believe about who we are and why we're here is wrong. Religion, philosophy, the transmutation of the soul, none of it is anything more than noise.

WOMAN: Oh, I get it! This is one of those deals where science and religion don't agree. You put a bounty on this guy, right?

MAN: What?

WOMAN: Your group—no, your *cult*—sent you to snuff him out and you couldn't do it. No, you *did* do it, but just before he croaked you realized he was right and that you had been used by the cult members and—

MAN: Could I finish, please?

[*She stares at him, nearly vibrating with expectation.*]

It was... I just felt bad because of it, OK? Nothing else. I never met him, he didn't do anything to me. All I did was read his book and it made everything seem... pointless.

WOMAN: Germs did?

MAN: Not germs. Watching all creation exploding like a billion billion Pop Rocks right before your eyes, and realizing you're as random and insignificant as a single one of those sparks.

WOMAN: Pop Rocks don't have sparks. They're candy.

MAN: Sparklers then. A billion billion sparklers.

WOMAN: Sparklers don't explode. [*He stares at her.*] I'm sorry, but it's true.

MAN: Fine, fine, argue with everything I say, but if you could grasp what it was he was getting at, if you could see it as clearly as I do, then you'd know that feeling hopeless isn't just when something bad happens. Or when you can't have something you want. You'd understand that knowledge all by itself could drive you to the edge of despair. That an intellectual crisis could be as bad as anything else life could dish out.

WOMAN: So tell me.

MAN: Pardon?

WOMAN: Explain it to me so I *do* understand.

MAN: I... You already have enough to worry about. I don't want to make it worse.

WOMAN: No, I really want to hear it. It'll be nice to know that the things I've been feeling bad about aren't really so terrible.

MAN: Yeah, but not everyone gets it. Lots of people read the same thing and—

WOMAN: Try me.

[*Pause.*]

Well?

MAN: It's complicated, see?

[*Pause. She waits.*]

It'd take a lot of time, and it's almost dark now.

WOMAN: You can't do it, can you?

MAN: What?

WOMAN: You can't explain it to me.

MAN: I most certainly can, it's just... Well, he uses so many technical examples to explain his point.

WOMAN: Like baseball.

MAN: Yes.

WOMAN: I understand baseball.

MAN: But there's lots more. Horses.

[*Pause.*]

And drunks. Drunks staggering up to a curb.

[*Pause.*]

And the bacteria thing. Bacteria and trees, and which weighs more.

WOMAN: You have some nerve.

MAN: Now wait a second...

WOMAN: Intellectual crisis my eye!

MAN: Look, just because I can't repeat it doesn't mean it didn't affect me, OK? When I *did* read it, I understood it fine, which means that if I went back and read it again I'd have the same reaction to it, which means I can know life is meaningless without actually being able to say why.

WOMAN: Stop, you're casting a shadow across my soul.

MAN: Look, I'll get you a copy. See for yourself.

WOMAN: Actually, I'm surprised he was even able to write the thing in the first place. Seems like once he had figured out how tiny and random he was, he would've nose-dived straight into the Charles.

MAN: Hah! Fat chance.

WOMAN: What's that mean?

MAN: That means that there's no way he's going anywhere.

WOMAN: But why not? He must know better than anyone how nothing matters, right? Well, except for you, of course. And he might even be able to articulate some of it.

MAN: Yeah, but people like him just don't.

WOMAN: Don't what? Kill themselves?

MAN: That's right. You don't have a great job and a bunch of books you wrote and a nice house and probably a wife and maybe some kids and lots of money and a car with leather seats and a monster engine and a great watch and twenty pairs of pants and really cool sunglasses, and then just go and check out on all that.

WOMAN: But he would know that there was nothing but a black void to look forward to.

MAN: Right. All the more reason to hunker down in your beach house and try like hell to live forever. No, I'll tell you when you check out. When your life is so crappy you embarrass yourself just thinking about it, but you keep at it because you figure it must be "For A Reason," it must be "Meant To Be," and then you go and read some rich idiot's book telling you how you're really just some tick on the ass of an evolutionary elephant, and there you go! What's left?! No family, no money, your last girlfriend so long ago that you can't even fantasize about her anymore without feeling guilty because she's too young for you now. And you look at—

WOMAN: But she'd be older too.

MAN: What?

WOMAN: Your girlfriend. Wouldn't she be older as well?

MAN: Yeah, but I don't remember her that way. Anyway, there it is. You add everything up worth living for and you get a negative number. Like your life was a credit card and you're looking at bankruptcy. *That's* when you do the nose-dive. Right at that exact second.

WOMAN: How much older?

MAN: Excuse me?

WOMAN: How much older are you now than she was then?

MAN: I don't... What does that have to do with anything?

WOMAN: I just want to get an idea of what you think is too old.

MAN: Why on earth would you care in the slightest?

WOMAN: It's one of those things people have different opinions on.

[*Pause.*]

Look, if you don't want to tell me, that's your business. But you did bring it up.

MAN: Not to talk about.

WOMAN: Fine. Whatever. You were saying.

MAN: What?

WOMAN: Before we got off the subject.

[*Pause.*]

MAN: I don't know. I can't remember now.

[*Pause.*]

It's eleven years, by the way.

WOMAN: You haven't had a girlfriend in eleven years?

MAN: No! I'm eleven years older now than she was then.

WOMAN: Oh. That's not so much. How much older than her were you when you broke up?

MAN: If I tell you that then you'll know how long it's been since I've seen someone.

WOMAN: But you have nothing to live for and want to end it all. What do you care?

MAN: Just because I want to die doesn't mean I want to give up my dignity.

WOMAN: You might want to take off those ankle weights before you say that.

[*He turns away.*]

Aw, come on. It was a joke. Tell me.

MAN: No.

WOMAN: Tell me. Please?

[*Pause.*]

MAN: Six years.

WOMAN: Since you've been with anyone? That's a long time.

MAN: No, since... See, I knew you'd get it twisted around and make me look bad. No, I was six years *older* than her when we broke up.

WOMAN: Oh. So it's only been five years.

MAN: Right.

WOMAN: Well that's nothing. Anything under six is acceptable. Was she nice?

MAN: Sure.

WOMAN: Pretty?

MAN: Very. Like a painting.

WOMAN: Painting of what?

MAN: Of a pretty woman.

WOMAN: And you miss her?

MAN: Not anymore.

WOMAN: You said you fantasize about her.

MAN: No, I said I can't because I feel guilty.

WOMAN: But you can only feel guilty if you do, so you must. What was she like?

MAN: I don't know. Regular, I guess.

WOMAN: Just how a woman wants to be described.

MAN: No, I meant not special in any way.

WOMAN: Then what do you fantasize about?

   [*Pause.*]

   What?

MAN: She was funny.

WOMAN: Uh-huh.

MAN: And smart. Always reading.

WOMAN: You fantasize about her reading?

MAN: I remember it, yeah. And being in her apartment. And her being in mine. And ordering pizza and staying in bed watching TV. And her starting to say something and my knowing what it was even before the words came out. And her listing all my faults and calling me a jerk and doing it with this smile that made it seem like she was saying she loved everything about me.

WOMAN: So why did you break up?

MAN: That's personal.

WOMAN: I know. Everything we're talking about is personal.

MAN: That's true.

[*Pause.*]

I had a problem with her cat.

WOMAN: Uh-oh.

MAN: He pissed in my hamper when she was staying with me. And I sort of gave her an ultimatum about it.

WOMAN: Bad move.

MAN: I didn't know. And she was gone so fast I barely had a chance to apologize.

WOMAN: So it's been hard then.

MAN: Hard?

WOMAN: Without her.

MAN: I don't know. It was better with her, I'll tell you that. And the cat would have died eventually.

WOMAN: Did you think about her today?

MAN: I think about her every day.

WOMAN: When you were going off the bridge?

MAN: Sure. I mean, not just her. The bacteria stuff mostly. But she sort of flickered there for a second.

WOMAN: Mm.

[*Pause.*]

You know, that sounds suspiciously like romantic sulking.

MAN: No, it's... No. See, I knew you'd think that if I told you. I was not jumping because of *her*, all right? I would have done it a long time ago if she were the reason.

WOMAN: But what if she hadn't left? Would you still be doing it?

MAN: How should I know? I might never have even read that book.

WOMAN: But if you had—if you read it and she were at home waiting for you with a pizza and a movie—would you still do it?

[*Pause. He looks off.*]

MAN: I don't...

[*Pause.*]

I think that kind of intellectual crisis mostly happens to people who don't have girlfriends they're nuts about.

WOMAN: I see.

[*Pause. They sit a moment.*]

So what now?

MAN: Oh. Well, I didn't bring a car because I didn't think I'd be going back, but if you need me to I can drive yours to the emergency room.

WOMAN: That's fine, but I meant what's next for you? What are you going to do?

MAN: Oh. I don't know. Try something else, I guess.

WOMAN: Oh.

MAN: Or maybe wait to see if we get some rain. I kind of had my heart set on the bridge thing.

WOMAN: You might want to try a bigger bridge this time.

MAN: I would, but this is the only one around.

WOMAN: Heck, go somewhere. Drive down to New York. They have lots of bridges there. You could get a hotel, see a show. Make a weekend of it.

MAN: But wouldn't that ruin the weekend if I knew I was going to jump right after?

WOMAN: It might. But it might make it better, too. I'd say you're in uncharted waters with that one.

MAN: I guess.

[*Pause.*]

What about you?

WOMAN: Me?

MAN: What are your plans?

WOMAN: I don't know. Everything got thrown off for me.

MAN: How?

WOMAN: I had this thing I wanted to do, and now I'm not sure when I'll be able to do it.

MAN: Tell me.

WOMAN: I'd rather not.

MAN: Come on. Maybe I can help.

[*He waits. She smiles at him. She then removes a small box from her pocket.*]

WOMAN: I was going to throw this into the river.

MAN: What is it, a ring?

WOMAN: A ring box, yes.

MAN: But not the ring?

WOMAN: I thought about it for a while and decided that it would be a sin to throw something of real value away. And since the box is technically what he presented me with, it would be fine if I just tossed that.

MAN: Oh. That makes sense.

WOMAN: But I throw with my right hand.

MAN: Oh.

[*Pause.*]

I could do it for you.

WOMAN: No.

MAN: It'd get there same as if you did it.

WOMAN: But I wouldn't be doing it myself.

MAN: But you'd be seeing to it that it got done. It'd be just as good.

WOMAN: I don't think that's how it works.

MAN: We don't know how it works. We're in uncharted waters here.

[*Pause.*]

WOMAN: All right then. Chuck away.

[*He takes the box from her. He then hops on his good leg a couple of steps and launches it far out towards the water. A satisfying "plunk" reaches them.*]

Thank you.

MAN: You're welcome. Feel better?

WOMAN: I don't know yet. I'll give it some time. You ready to go?

MAN: Sure.

WOMAN: Maybe I should be helping you.

MAN: I'll be OK.

WOMAN: At least to the car. Here. Lean on me.

[*He hesitates.*]

Go ahead, I'm strong.

[*He places his hand on her shoulder, balancing. They make their way slowly.*]

MAN: So you think maybe now you won't have to... you know...

WOMAN: What?

MAN: If you're feeling better about the whole thing.

WOMAN: You mean killing myself?

MAN: Yeah.

WOMAN: What, you think I change my mind that easy?

MAN: I'm not saying—

WOMAN: Toss away one little ring box and everything I'm feeling just flies away with it?

MAN: No, I just thought... I mean, if you wanted to... I thought I might try that New York trip you suggested.

WOMAN: Oh.

[*Guiding him up the bank.*]

Careful.

MAN: Thanks. And I thought, if you wanted, if it wasn't too weird or any-thing—because I know it's this big personal thing—but if you wanted...

WOMAN: [*Stopping; looking at him.*] Are you asking me to jump with you?

MAN: Only if it was something you thought would work for you. I mean, I know bridges aren't for everyone.

WOMAN: No, the bridge is fine. I'm just not sure when I'll be doing it, is all.

[*As they resume walking.*]

MAN: It could be any time. You could call me and let me know.

WOMAN: What about seeing a show?

MAN: Yeah, I think that's a great idea. And a ball game, a museum, any-thing you wanted.

WOMAN: I don't know. I'll have to think about it.

[*Pause.*]

But it might be nice.

[*As they disappear from sight.*]

MAN: And I could lend you my copy of that book if you're interested.

WOMAN: Good, I'd like that. I read a lot, you know.

[*Lights.*]

END OF PLAY

WEST OF STUPID

Cusi Cram

West of Stupid by Cusi Cram. Copyright © 2002 by Cusi Cram. All rights
reserved.

CAUTION: *West of Stupid*, being duly copyrighted, is subject to a royalty. All
performance rights are controlled by Sarah Jane Leigh, c/o ICM. No professional or non-professional performance of the play may be given without obtain-
ing in advance the written permission of Sarah Jane Leigh, c/o ICM, and paying
the requisite fee. Inquiries concerning all rights should be addressed to Sarah
Jane Leigh, c/o ICM, 40 West 57th Street, New York, New York 10019.

Cusi Cram

CUSI CRAM is of Bolivian and Scottish descent. Her plays include *Landlocked* (South Coast Rep Hispanic Playwrights Project/Pacific Playwrights Festival and The Miranda Theater), *The End of It all* (South Coast Rep Hispanic Playwrights Project/Pacific Playwrights Festival), *Lucy and the Conquest* (Juilliard and The O'Neill Playwrights Conference), *Fuente* (The Cherry Lane Alternative), and two solo shows, which she also performs, *Bolivia* and *Euripidames* (New Georges). Her plays have also been developed and performed at MCC, The Williamstown Theater Festival, Naked Angels, Joe's Pub at the Public Theater, The Women's Project, Here, The Lark Theater, P.S. 122, and The Dag Hamerskjold Theater at the United Nations. She is a recipient of a fellowship and residency from the Lila Acheson American Playwrights Program at Juilliard, a residency at Marymount College, and the Le Comte du Nuoy Prize from the Lincoln Center Theater Foundation. She has been commissioned by South Coast Repertory, New Georges, and Theatreworks USA. She is a member of MCC's Playwrights Coalition and New Georges' "kitchen cabinet." She writes for the children's television program "Arthur" and has been nominated for an Emmy and a Humanitas award for her work on the show. Ms. Cram is a graduate of Brown University. She lives in Greenwich Village with her husband, Peter Hirsch.

CHARACTERS:

JUNE, in her early 50s
JEFF, in his late 20s

SETTING:

A café in campo di Fiori, Rome

JUNE: A fool. That's what I am. My mother had a phrase... what was it... west of stupid. That's what she used to call me. Well, she was right. God.

JEFF: I don't get it, Gram's phrase.

JUNE: She had another one, I liked... dumb as a doughnut. Maybe it was dense as a doughnut? I am not a phrase turner. It's probably a math thing. I bet people who are good at math are good at that sort of thing.

JEFF: Why are you a fool?

JUNE: What? Oh... I forget. There's this strange fogginess. It comes and goes. But I know... I know I had discovered something, something that pointed to my utter and complete idiocy.

JEFF: You shouldn't talk like that. You... you put yourself down.

JUNE: Shut up, Jeffrey. [*Longish pause, some sipping.*] It's the coffee that makes me feel west of stupid.

JEFF: The coffee?

JUNE: Because... because it tastes so goddamn good. Because for seven years I've been driving every Saturday to Essex to the Bean There, that's spelt B-E-A-N and this woman Peg, Peg makes me a cappuccino and I look out the window at all the white houses and all the white people and tell Peg she makes a spectacular four dollar cup of coffee. But now... now that I know what I've been missing, the years of savory that have escaped me, I feel like punching Peg and scalding her with every single cup of rotten coffee she's ever made me.

JEFF: You told me once you enjoyed the drive to Essex.

JUNE: I never said that. That's just something you want to think I said.

JEFF: What do you mean by that?

JUNE: Never mind, dear. Never mind. I feel so happy at the thought of scalding Peg. I don't want things to turn. The mood. This place. This place. There's so much life... so much life in this room, I wish I could bottle it and drink it. I am so happy I never learnt Italian because all of these people are probably talking about carburetors and insurance but it looks like... like... everybody is talking about fucking.

JEFF: [*A little uncomfortable.*] Didn't you take Italian lessons?

JUNE: The teacher, the teacher, was a small woman.

JEFF: What does that mean, Mom?

JUNE: Does it matter, Jeff, my Italian teacher at the Old Saybrook YMCA?

JEFF: I guess not.

JUNE: [*Pointing to a man.*] Do you think he's a soldier? He looks like a soldier. I tell you, I'm not sure what it is but I find the soldiers in Italy to be so sexy. Back home, if someone is in a uniform, it sort of makes me ignore them automatically, you know? But did you see the guard at Fiumicino? He held his gun... in this way that... well Jeff, it looked positively pornographic. Did you see him?

JEFF: I missed him. What was small about her, I mean specifically? I'd like to know.

JUNE: Oh, God. Sometimes you're a real downer. I guess you don't get to fantasize about my soldier.

JEFF: I guess not.

JUNE: Mrs. Franchetti, my Italian teacher at the Old Saybrook Y, took great offense at my comments. And though I had never been to Italy, I had read about it and that threatened Mrs. Franchetti, who had been here on two package tours. I've been a teacher most of my life, Jeff, and I knew that even though Mrs. Franchetti spoke Italian adequately, that it would not be possible for me to learn it from her because she was not a generous woman. She was small in her outlook on life, small in her desires. Mrs. Franchetti lived at a certain decibel of miserable smallness, which she had accepted as all right. Mrs. Franchetti was full of fear and doubt had no philosophy or poetry in her and therefore I could not learn the language of Dante from her.

JEFF: Then why take Italian at the Y? Why not drive to New Haven or Hartford, or somewhere else, where someone "large" might teach.

JUNE: I don't think this is about Mrs. Franchetti. What is this about, Jeffrey?

JEFF: It's about trying to get some clarity, some understanding, Mother. Your sailing teacher was small, so were your pottery, tai chi, massage, and oil painting teachers. Your neighbors are small. Everyone who works at Old Saybrook High is small. My hockey coach, my violin teacher, all my babysitters, every best friend I ever had, what did they have in common? Smallness, according to you. Pretty much anyone you call a friend is small and has no poetry or philosophy in them. Are there no large poetic and philosophical people in the entire state of Connecticut, Mom?

JUNE: In my opinion, very few.

[*A long pause.*]

JUNE: [*Pointing to someone.*] Look at him, will you?

JEFF: Don't point. Pointing is rude in any language.

JUNE: I bet he has a huge dick.

JEFF: Excuse me?

JUNE: Gianormous, I bet. His hands are thick. I took a palm reading class in Mystic and the teacher, Aroshn, by the way she was the opposite of small, and she shared some very interesting facts with me. Fleshy hands, fleshy hands mean you are a sensual being, Jeff, that's what Aroshn said.

JEFF: What kind of a name is Aroshn?

JUNE: Her name was Sharon. She just switched the letters around. Isn't that clever?

JEFF: It sounds like erosion. What would my name be, Fefj?

JUNE: [*Looking toward the man.*] You know, since I got the news, I think and dream about sex all the time. I tell you, the orgasms I've been having in my sleep are so vivid and so much better than anything I ever had in real life, I wake up quivering. And if I think about the dream, I can still feel some of the pleasure. It's a nice side effect.

JEFF: [*Very very uncomfortable.*] Oh. Well, good. Good, I guess if it makes you feel better?

JUNE: In the last five years, I've lost interest in sex.

JEFF: Mom, do we have to talk about this?

JUNE: I can talk about whatever I want, Jeff. It has to do with gravity, my loss of interest. 'Cause if you think about it, good sex is all about buoyancy, everything being plump and full. And no matter what you do, as you get older you just can't keep things buoyant naturally. I find this loss... loss of buoyancy in myself and others unstimulating. But in my dreams, in my dreams, I am just bouncing like a goddamn beach ball and everyone else is too. [*Doing a clandestine point.*] He seems *very* buoyant to me.

JEFF: He could speak English, Mom.

[*A pause.* JEFF *looks at his hands. He pinches the flesh.* JUNE *notices and smiles.*]

JUNE: What's he drinking? That red drink, what's that red drink?

JEFF: Bitters, I think. It comes from artichokes or pomegranates, I forget which.

JUNE: Be a lamb and get me one. [*Whispering.*] Just like the buoyant guy is having.

[JEFF *gets up and crosses upstage to the bar.* JUNE *tries to stifle a cough into a handkerchief. She has a hard time.* JEFF *returns with a drink.*]

JEFF: Mom? Mom? Are you all right, Mom?

JUNE: [*Coughing.*] Fit as a fiddle. It's just the cigarette smoke. [*She stops coughing.*] I love Italy. They must not have cancer here, the way everyone just smokes everywhere. It's beautiful. [*A little cough.*]

JEFF: Do you want the spray?

JUNE: God, no. [*Beat.*] You're clenching your jaw, Jeff. It's got to be bad for you and it reminds me of your father. I don't want to think about your father in Rome.

JEFF: [*Clenching his jaw.*] I'm not clenching.

JUNE: What's wrong? You clench when something's wrong.

JEFF: I was thinking about Mrs. Franchetti.

JUNE: Killjoy.

JEFF: Mom, you said, you said, that you would come on this trip, if I promised to not be polite. You said that.

JUNE: Be my guest.

JEFF: OK.

JUNE: You're still clenching. Can you be rude and not clench?

JEFF: Mom!

JUNE: Sorry!

JEFF: Well... Well, you're this really large person, Mom and it seems, it seems to me that most of your life you... you've put yourself in these small situations... so... so you can feel all large and outraged.

JUNE: [*Angrily.*] Is that what I've done? From your birds-eye view, up there on your high pony pony horse that's how you see it?

JEFF: I just want to understand why.

JUNE: Well, it's hard to understand someone you never see. [*Beat.*] I understand, Jeff. I'm not a success. I'm not rich. I'm not healthy. I am a divorced Connecticut schoolteacher with a temper. Your father...

JEFF: This is not about Dad.

JUNE: But it is. We look to our parents as examples and ever since you left home, you've wanted nothing to do with me. Every time I see you, your jaw is clenched and you can't look me in the eye because you're afraid if you do, you might see yourself. And you know what? It doesn't matter a bit. Because I love you, honey. I love you right through all your disapproval because I knew you when you were kind and afraid of things under your bed. I knew you when you couldn't fall asleep unless I held you. And that kind of knowing lasts forever.

[*JUNE holds* JEFF'*s hand to her heart. A moment. An alarm goes off on* JEFF'*s watch.*]

JUNE: Oh, Jesus. What's that?

JEFF: [*Collecting himself.*] It's time for... for your pills.

[*JEFF begins to unpack several bottles of pills from his knapsack and place them on the table.*]

JUNE: I wish... I wish we didn't have to do that here. The soldier will see.

JEFF: The timing is very important, Mom.

JUNE: Jeffie?

JEFF: [*Counting pills, looking at instructions.*] Just a sec, this is complicated

JUNE: I didn't like Mrs. Franchetti because she was... she was just like me. I want to die large.

JEFF: What are you talking about, Mom?

JUNE: I never traveled before because I knew... I knew that if I went to other places and saw people like that soldier with the fleshy hands and drank artichoke juice, I would see the smallness of Old Saybrook and then I would have to do something and I was afraid of the something... I don't want to be afraid anymore, Jeff. I don't want to take my pills. I don't want experimental treatments in New Haven. I don't want to go back to Connecticut. Ever. I want to die in Rome, dreaming of transcendent orgasms.

JEFF: But... Mom, there's hope. Dr. Greisman said, he said there's some hope.

JUNE: There is, Jeff, just not the kind you're talking about. I am hopeful that my death at the Hassler Hotel, overlooking the Spanish Steps, with my son by my side will be joyful and filled with hope.

JEFF: That's not what this trip was about. I wanted to give you things, things you've never let yourself have, good food and wine and paintings and views that would break your heart. I wanted to show you a place where people have mastered living, so you would fight to live like this, so you would fight to come back here. I gave you Rome because I wanted you to fight, Mom.

JUNE: I can't win this, honey. But I am so grateful that you made me come here. I just want to stay. I want to die in Rome of consumption like a Henry James heroine. Do you think consumption was like 19th century cancer?

JEFF: I dunno. It sure sounds better, though.

JUNE: It does.

[JEFF *is silent.* JUNE *reaches for her glass of bitters. She lifts the drink to* JEFF's *lips.*]

JUNE: It'll make you feel better. It tastes like medicine.

[JEFF *drinks a few sips.*]

JEFF: It's disgusting.

JUNE: But such a festive color.

JEFF: I think it's for digestion.

JUNE: I could use a snack. It looks like they have sandwiches. Should I get some? [*Whispering.*] It could be my moment to talk to the buoyant soldier with the huge hands. Just look at them, Jeff, they are *abnormally* large.

JEFF: They're gianormous.

JUNE: I think they have spinach and mozzarella. Sound good?

JEFF: Whatever you want Mom, whatever you want.

[JUNE *gets up, turns her back, and walks toward the bar. She turns around and looks at* JEFF. JEFF *slowly and methodically puts the pills in his knapsack.* JUNE *watches him.* JEFF *finishes and looks out to the piazza.* JUNE *also looks out to somewhere beyond the piazza and smiles.*]

END OF PLAY

THE SUMMER SUBLET

Laurence Klavan

The Summer Sublet by Laurence Klavan. Copyright © 2002 Laurence Klavan.
All rights reserved.

CAUTION: Professionals and amateurs are hereby warned that *The Summer Sublet* by Laurence Klavan is subject to a royalty. It is fully protected under the copyright laws of the United States of America, and of all countries covered by the International Copyright Union (including the Dominion of Canada and the rest of the British Commonwealth), and of all countries covered by the Pan-American Copyright Convention and the Universal Copyright Convention, and of all countries with which the United States has reciprocal copyright relations. All rights, including professional, amateur, motion picture, recitation, lecturing, public reading, radio broadcasting, television, video or sound taping, all other forms of mechanical or electronic reproduction, such as information storage and retrieval systems and photo-copyright, and the rights of translation into foreign languages are strictly reserved. Particular emphasis is laid upon the question of readings, permission for which must be secured from the author's agent in writing.
Inquiries concerning all performing rights to the play should be addressed to the author's agent, Ronald Gwiazda, ROSENSTONE/WENDER, 38 East 29th Street, New York, New York 10016.

Laurence Klavan

LAURENCE KLAVAN received two Drama Desk nominations for the book and lyrics to *Bed and Sofa*, the musical produced by the Vineyard Theater in New York. It also received two Obie Awards, five other Drama Desk nominations (including Best Musical), and an Outer Critics Circle nomination as Best Musical. It has been published by Dramatists Play Service, recorded by Varese Sarabande, and subsequently produced by the Wilma Theatre in Philadelphia, where it won two Barrymore Awards.

His full-length play *The Magic Act* was produced by the Ensemble Studio Theatre and published by Dramatists Play Service. He was featured in *Miami Stories: Bellow, Malamud, and Klavan*, produced by the American Jewish Theater. His one-acts, including *Freud's House, Sleeping Beauty, Smoke, If Walls Could Talk, The Show Must Go On*, and *Gorgo's Mother*, have been produced by Ensemble Studio Theatre, Manhattan Punch Line, Working Theatre, Actors Theater of Louisville, People's Light & Theater Co., Philadelphia Festival Theatre for New Plays, among others, and published by Dramatists Play Service. He has been awarded a grant from the National Endowment for the Arts and has received commissions from the Actors Theatre of Louisville, the Vineyard Theatre, and, most recently, the Wilma Theater, where he is writing the musical *Embarrassments* with composer Polly Pen.

He wrote the screenplay *One Bedroom* for Tri-Star Pictures, *The Unusual Suspects* for Warner Brothers, and his original screenplay *Mr. Nice Guy* was optioned by Viacom. His work for children's television includes *Corduroy* on the USA Network and the syndicated *Adventures of Superboy*, and he was featured as part of the "HBO New Writers Project." He recently wrote the cable film *Me and Jezebel* for the American Movie Classics network, and is developing the screenplay *Disobedience* with director Tony Gerber for Killer Films.

His novel *Mrs. White*, written under a pseudonym, won the Edgar Award from the Mystery Writers of America and was made into the film *White of the Eye*. His novel *I Watch Lois* was published by Pinnacle Books. His short plays and stories have been published in *Playgirl* magazine, *Ellery Queen's Mystery Magazine*, and elsewhere.

He lives in New York City.

The Summer Sublet was produced in the Ensemble Studio Theatre 2001 Marathon of One-Act Plays in New York City. It was directed by Keith Reddin and featured Ebon Moss-Bachrach, Elizabeth Hanly Rice, and Greg Stuhr.

CHARACTERS:

LLOYD
BERNICE
FRANK
VOICES OF: OTHER MAN
             MAN #2

[*We hear, as if coming up through the floorboards—*]

WOMAN'S VOICE: Shut up, you fat fuck! I'm just trying to help you!

MAN'S VOICE: Keep your Goddamn voice down, you'll wake the fucking baby!

WOMAN'S VOICE: Since when do you care? That's the biggest load of bullshit yet!

MAN'S VOICE: You want to hit me? Go ahead and Goddamn hit me!

WOMAN'S VOICE: I'll knock you into an outer borough, you flabby piece of crap!

[*Lights rise, dimly, on a small studio apartment in a brownstone, virtually unfurnished: a bed, a desk, a kitchenette. LLOYD, early 20s, is asleep in bed. It is very early morning.*]

MAN'S VOICE: It'll be hard to hit me with a broken arm, baby!

WOMAN'S VOICE: Just fucking try it! You'll be in handcuffs so fast— if they can fit them around your fat man's wrists!

[*Slowly, awakened by the yelling, LLOYD crawls out of bed. Through the rest, he dresses. The sound of a baby crying.*]

MAN'S VOICE: Now look what you Goddamn did!

WOMAN'S VOICE: Me? Who's the one who's been screaming like a stucking pig?!

MAN'S VOICE: A stucking pig?! Good going!

WOMAN'S VOICE: I meant a fucking pig, you know what I Goddamn meant!

MAN'S VOICE: Shut up!

[He has finished dressing. Full lights on apartment now. LLOYD *stands beside* BERNICE. *She is in her early 30s, wearing overalls, a tool belt and a cap. They look at the wall.]*

BERNICE: Wow. It actually buckled the walls a little bit.

LLOYD: I told you.

BERNICE: You wouldn't think that just a little water—

LLOYD: A "little" is hardly how I'd—

BERNICE: —that a tiny little leak would—

LLOYD: This seems like a whole faucet overflowed—that it came to the top of a tub, and—I thought somebody might be, you know...

[Gestures.]

BERNICE: What?

[Beat, realizing.]

Killing themselves?

LLOYD: Yes. You know. In the tub. Wrists slashed. Eyes rolled back. Water running. Dead.

[She just looks at him.]

BERNICE: Have you been, like, a little depressed lately?

LLOYD: No. Who, me? I've—heard things, that's all.

BERNICE: Like, what, weeping, or whatever?

LLOYD: No. Shouting. Oaths and epithets. "You fat" so-and-so. "You big piece of" this-and-that. Top of their lungs. Crack of dawn. Enough to make anyone—

BERNICE: *Kill* themselves?

LLOYD: Yes.

[BERNICE *shakes her head.*]

BERNICE: Jesus. You've even got nice names for euphemisms. Get close to those words, buddy, they won't bite.

LLOYD: [*Annoyed.*] Thanks for the advice. Now, what are you going to do about the damage?

BERNICE: Look, before you condescend, understand what's above and beneath you. The water was from upstairs. The screaming was from down. Okay?

LLOYD: Really? So, you heard it, too?

BERNICE: While I was screaming it. "You fat fucking" so-and-so. That was me.

[*He stares at her.*]

LLOYD: Really? Wow, I could have sworn... from the way it shook the bed, that it came from... It was like I was stuck in a snow globe—with no snow, of course—but being buffeted back and forth, back and forth, by two big voices, and—

BERNICE: It was a spirited exchange of ideas between two opinionated adults who wake up to work for a living. Unlike some others.

[*Beat. Defensively...*]

LLOYD: I'm about to look for work. I'm just here until September, remember? I'm just out of school. This is my friend's place, who's off to teach in Morocco.

BERNICE: Oh, right. I remembered September but forgot about the rest.

LLOYD: Don't bother, because it doesn't matter. Because he's not coming back. Not because he's dead, but because he's moving. These are the last two months on his lease.

BERNICE: I never assumed he was dead.

LLOYD: Oh. Right.

[*Beat. Shaking her head,* BERNICE *inspects the wall. Trying to laugh it off...*]

LLOYD: Look, it's not like I care about you and your husband. You two just woke me up, that's all.

BERNICE: Well, it's kind of in your best interest if your landlords love each other, isn't it?

LLOYD: I just meant—it's your problem, it's personal.

BERNICE: Who said Frank and I have a problem? But it's one thing to complain, it's another not to care. Just as a general rule.

LLOYD: I care, I care, okay?

BERNICE: Good. I'll keep that in my pocket for when I need to know.

[LLOYD *looks at her, curiously.* BERNICE *breaks this by checking out the rest of the place, hugging herself.*]

BERNICE: Eek. You like it arctic, don't you? Your own little igloo.

LLOYD: Well, it *is* July—

BERNICE: And I really ought to do something about that kitchen cabinet.

LLOYD: Don't bother. Really.

BERNICE: It doesn't annoy you? It would drive me nuts.

LLOYD: No, I just open the other one and reach all the way around. It gets a bit raw where it rubs the underside of my skin, but a little lotion, and it doesn't even hurt so much.

[*Digesting this,* BERNICE *looks out the window.*]

BERNICE: And that's some view, I forget.

LLOYD: It's fine.

BERNICE: All those hearses can't be so hot.

LLOYD: Well, when they bring the body bags in, it's a little—disconcerting. But I find if I turn completely to the side, I only catch a glimpse, and then I just stand by the sink until it's over.

BERNICE: And get the dishes done?

LLOYD: Exactly.

[*Dismissing this, she starts out.*]

BERNICE: I'll be back with some rods. Or else just staple a sheet.

LLOYD: You don't have to—there's really no reason—I mean—why fix things up if I'm only moving out in the fall?

[*She stops at the door.*]

BERNICE: Everybody's a renter, bud. In the big picture, nobody buys.

[*He looks at her again.*]

LLOYD: You're a special kind of a super, aren't you?

BERNICE: Yeah. I'm a wise and lovable leprechaun. That's me. A little gnome with a nail gun.

LLOYD: Exactly.

BERNICE: So go about your business. You'll hardly know I'm here.

[*She is gone. Calling after her...*]

LLOYD: I'll probably be out, anyway, looking for a job... In fact, I'm just on my way out now, so....

[*Beat. But he doesn't go anywhere. He sits on the bed. Then he lies down, tries to sleep again. Lights dim. Then—from downstairs—*]

FRANK'S VOICE: I'm telling you for once and fucking all, Bernice, get off my Goddamn back!

BERNICE'S VOICE: You act like I'm not even involved—who's gonna get hurt when the shit hits the fan?!

FRANK'S VOICE: Oh, "when" and not "if"—like it's a given it'll all go wrong—thanks for the confidence, castrating cow!

BERNICE'S VOICE: Well, don't come running to me—if your feet aren't too fucking fat to run!

[*Awakened*, LLOYD *crawls out of bed again. Lights start to rise.*]

LLOYD: So my girlfriend stopped eating. Not entirely, of course, but just enough to send a scare through everyone. Eventually, she started to get that skeleton look, and it's—I mean, there are so many illnesses that attack you uninvited, to actually—ask—to endanger your life, like choosing to choke on a chicken bone, escapes my understanding. What's the big idea? You don't even get the fun of driving fast before you, you know, slam into a train. I know they say it's a control thing, that this you can control because you feel so out of control in everything else—but what about the other people? There're only so many ways you can press a sandwich on someone. By the end, I would have, you know, put a funnel on her face and force-fed her, as foolish as that may sound, but again, to no avail. The awful, awful helplessness.

[*When the lights have risen fully,* BERNICE *is in the middle of the floor, hard at work, fixing the cabinet door. A stroller stands in a corner.* LLOYD *has been addressing her.*]

LLOYD: The funny thing is, after we—parted ways—I saw her across campus, and she looked just fine, had filled out, as if she had just been waiting for me to—what? Stop caring? Okay, well, I did, I have. So, push the plate away, anyone else, and see what reaction you get. You have an ailment or any, any kind of issue, and you are on your own! There is nothing, nothing that I can do for you now!

[*Beat.*]

BERNICE: Pass me that thing-a-ma-hoop, will you?

LLOYD: Sure.

[*He does. She uses it.*]

BERNICE: Well, at least you came to the right conclusion.

[*Beat. From the stroller, the baby cries.*]

LLOYD: You're kidding me, right?

BERNICE: Hey, I can see all that college paid off.

[BERNICE *has gone over and, discreetly, started to breast-feed.*]

LLOYD: See? That's what I mean. If you wouldn't have fed her, it would be an abomination.

BERNICE: Yeah, but I wouldn't empty my entire hooter in her head, either.

LLOYD: That's a very delicate distinction. And who is she to dictate anyway, the one with no proper judgment at this particular juncture?

BERNICE: Mara's an infant. Your friend was at least a, what, a senior?

LLOYD: Sophomore. And, anyway, that's my old idea, and one I am delighted to be disabused of. Disabused from? From which I am delighted to be—

BERNICE: Forget it. I only had one year at a state school.

LLOYD: Let her crawl to find her formula. That's my mantra now.

[BERNICE *looks at him.*]

BERNICE: Was that a sad attempt to shock me?

LLOYD: I don't seem sincere?

[*She finishes.*]

BERNICE: That kind of attitude will land you in prison, tough guy. And good luck with the more muscular men, because you're kind of cute.

[*She looks at him. But he does not pick up on it. Shrugging a little, she starts to go.*]

LLOYD: From what I heard last night, you should know about doing dangerous things.

[*She is at the door. She decides to ignore this.*]

BERNICE: I'll be back to stain your trim.

[LLOYD *just looks at her. Then... a bit faintly...*]

LLOYD: Well... you've got the key.

[*She leaves, closing the door. He waits a second. Then he lies back down on the bed once more, tries to sleep. Lights dim.*]

[*Then—waking him again, we hear another man's voice, yelling as if up to a window from outside—*]

OTHER MAN'S VOICE: Hey, Frankie! Frankie! Come on out and play, Frankie! Frank! What are you so afraid of, Frank? Why don't you come out? We know you're in there! Don't be shy, Frank! Don't be scared! We just want to talk to you! Don't make us beg! Okay... if that's the way you want it! But we'll be back! Don't think we'll forget you! Because we won't! We won't forget what you did! You back-stabbing piece of shit!

[LLOYD *has gotten up, rattled, looked out. When lights rise, he has met* BERNICE *in the doorway. She is carrying a new curtain on a rod.*]

LLOYD: Are you *okay?*

BERNICE: What do you mean? It's just the one flight with this—

LLOYD: No, I mean—you know, last night, the big bellowing outside the— the dangerous sounding dude with the—it was even worse than the usual shattering of glass in a garbage truck that always happens when they—

BERNICE: Oh. That.

[*She has hung the curtain.*]

BERNICE: Eek. I forgot the extension cord.

[*She starts out to the hall again.* LLOYD *calls after her, incredulous.*]

LLOYD: Well, he wasn't yelling for me, you know.

BERNICE'S VOICE: [*From the hall.*] You could have fooled me. But I guess over-reacting gives you a good reason, doesn't it?

[*She re-enters.*]

BERNICE: I mean, how can you look for work when you were kept awake for a little while last night? Keep hiding in bed here, honey, behind a broken heart. But remember that the rent comes due.

[*She is working again. Stung, striking back...*]

LLOYD: And will someone come calling for me the way they did for Frank?

[*No reply.*]

LLOYD: You said he was in the "rag trade." That sounds about right.

[*She will not be provoked.*]

LLOYD: You don't want to be one of those—wives.

[BERNICE *now looks up.*]

BERNICE: What do you mean?

LLOYD: You know, with the big hair and the anger, always being restrained in a courtroom. Or else, always kept in the dark, Diane Keaton with the door slammed in her face.

BERNICE: You mean...

[*Beat, realizing.*]

A *Mafia* wife?

LLOYD: Yes.

BERNICE: Jesus. Put the word in your mouth, kiddo, it won't come.

LLOYD: You don't want to be one of those, do you?

BERNICE: Even if I did want, it wouldn't ever happen. And stop saying that about Frank, he's at least once removed.

LLOYD: Oh, yeah? Well, whoever was outside last night came pretty close.

BERNICE: That was an emotional appeal from a very passionate person. Perhaps you wouldn't understand, but not everything can be an e-mail, sometimes you got to write an opera.

LLOYD: At 2 A.M.?

BERNICE: Your problem is you only trust the tame. You're afraid of the overblown. Don't be so afraid to embarrass yourself.

[*Annoyed, she starts out. Beat.* LLOYD *shrugs.*]

LLOYD: Okay.

[*Awkwardly, he gets in her way. Then he steps forward and kisses her. She looks at him. A bit shakily...*]

LLOYD: Well. You said.

[*Beat. Rattled, but not angry, just sighing at his bad timing...*]

BERNICE: It's a little late. I have to go down to dinner.

[*He is surprised by her reaction. She starts to go. Encouraged, blocking her way, flirtatiously—*]

LLOYD: And Frank can't be made to wait, right?

[*She puts her hand at his chest, stopping him.*]

BERNICE: A helpful hint—going further down that highway won't help you. Stick to stepping forward and kissing me again, that was pretty good.

[*Now invited, a bit more stiffly this time, he does so.*]

LLOYD: Sorry. I can see why they call it "spontaneity."

BERNICE: It's okay, it's okay, it was good, go again.

[*They are kissing deeply now. Then he pulls back.*]

LLOYD: I'm a little nervous—I mean, from my history. Does love solve *anything*?

BERNICE: [*Softly.*] It solves not being in love. And that's always enough.

LLOYD: Is it? [*Beat.*] Well... we'll see.

[Tugged closer, he keeps kissing her. Soon he is matching her aggression with his own. Lights fade. Lights rise on FRANK downstage, 30s, heavyset. In a suit. Opposite LLOYD.]

FRANK: Well, since you asked, I work in the garment industry. That's how come I can afford the apartment house. I do something that has to do with selling. But—

LLOYD: [*To himself.*] ...But it's too boring to pay attention to. Frank's going on at great length about it. Why did I think coming down to their place would help? And he's saying "fuck" a lot—every other word out of his mouth—what is it with some people? Of course, now they practically say it on TV. They're all a bunch of—

FRANK: —fucking schmattes! And I'm wondering—

LLOYD: Does Bernice wear his clothes? She usually just parades around in overalls. Is it her or is that just simply sexy? Is it, like, a little girl thing? Or just the way it hangs at the breasts and accentuates them? What a woman. She sure does look adorable in—

FRANK: —the Goddamn garment district! Everybody skims a little on the sly!

LLOYD: What was that, some kind of a clue? Nah, he's settling down again, but still laughing in a sort of threatening way. And he won't stop talking. Does he ever let anyone else get a word in edgewise? What does "edgewise" mean, anyway? An opening so small, another word would have to slide in from the side? Something so tight, that's sexy.

FRANK: —Don't look at me that way! What can a kid like you know?

LLOYD: Hey, he just spit on me, Christ! Does he suspect something? No, his head's too far up his ass. Is he armed? Is that bulge beneath his coat a gun or just, like, a fat man's breast? If I called the cops, what could they do? Is it too late to make a break? And then where would I go? I'd have to sneak back in for all my stuff. I come down here to get information, and I end up getting killed. Christ! I—

FRANK: —I can't control the world, this I can control, so stay out of my fucking shit! I've said it so often to Bernice!

LLOYD: Was *that* a clue? By thinking my own thoughts, did I just miss some key information? And, anyway, what can I do, ask him to go back?

FRANK: You better keep this all under your hat, you hear me?

LLOYD: [*Responding.*] I do. I do. I understand everything.

[FRANK *just looks at him, realizing…*]

FRANK: No, you don't. You haven't heard a word I've been saying.

LLOYD: [*Panicked.*] I haven't? No, I—

FRANK: It's all right. It's a relief. I'm just so used to being judged.

LLOYD: [*Relieved.*] Are you?

FRANK: [*Nods.*] Some women think that, if you make a mistake, that constant criticism will—they think that pounding on the machine will mean more candy. And all they get is their money back. If they're lucky.

LLOYD: [*Solemnly.*] Yeah.

[*He shakes* LLOYD's *hand.*]

FRANK: Thanks for not caring enough to have an opinion.

LLOYD: Sure.

FRANK: We're only on this earth a fleeting instant. Let's just enjoy our oh-so-brief time.

[*Beat.*]

Any more stuff broken, let Bernice know. Immediately.

[*He pats* LLOYD's *shoulder.* LLOYD *weakly smiles. As lights fade on exiting* FRANK *and shift back to the apartment,* LLOYD *starts to tiptoe there.* BERNICE *looks up from the bed, half-dressed.*]

BERNICE: Hey… where'd you go?

LLOYD: I'm right here.

BERNICE: [*Refers to his feet.*] What are you doing?

LLOYD: [*Whispers.*] Tiptoes tend to be—the floor is always—and we *are* right above—

BERNICE: [*Whispers in imitation.*] Not everyone hears a squeak and assumes it's the apocalypse, you know.

LLOYD: But we already—the bed—it's been moving in ways that didn't suggest home repair, and—

BERNICE: Frank would never figure on... It would never be... in his way of thought. Please feel free to press down on the heel of your foot.

LLOYD: Okay. Thank you.

[*He goes to the bed.*]

BERNICE: He has other... areas of expertise.

LLOYD: I see. I'm sorry.

BERNICE: Don't be. It's not the whole ball of wax. Frank's a little insecure about his sexual—stature. But I always tell him that, just like fruits and vegetables, sometimes the tiniest things taste the best.

LLOYD: Frank's a lucky man.

[*Downstairs, faint sound of baby crying.*]

BERNICE: Besides, can't you hear? He's babysitting.

[LLOYD *acknowledges this. Now he is fiddling with some tools, a hammer, he can't stay still.*]

BERNICE: And too much tension just makes you sweat.

LLOYD: Give me a break. I've never been a homewrecker before.

BERNICE: Maybe it's the no-air-conditioning.

LLOYD: You think? I still can't get used to it. It being August and all.

BERNICE: To me, it's an odd atmosphere, like the air on another planet. Let's have the humidity, I say. It won't last long, after all.

LLOYD: They say that someday, it will, that soon New York will be August all year long, no more seasons.

BERNICE: I know. It's unnatural. Like being young forever.

LLOYD: Well, *that* sounds nice, no?

BERNICE: Not if you still die. Then you'd die knowing nothing. Even a dog doesn't do that, he's gained a little wisdom from all his—walks, or whatever.

[LLOYD *just shrugs, unconvinced. She sees this.*]

BERNICE: Don't stay in the summer, that's all I'm saying. While everybody's putting on their parkas, you'll look strange in your shorts.

LLOYD: So getting older... is learning to accept sitting in the snow?

BERNICE: I can see that this is in one ear.

[LLOYD *waits a second. Then, proving it true, he hears something in the hall, goes towards it.*]

LLOYD: Hold on. Shh.

[BERNICE *sighs, shakes her head.*]

BERNICE: That's another good thing about getting older. You get less jumpy.

LLOYD: Do you?

BERNICE: [*Nods.*] You know more when to worry.

LLOYD: That'll be worth waiting for.

[*Beat.*]

What do you think Frank would do if he knew?

BERNICE: He can't fire me, I'm union.

[*Different tone.*]

He'd—believe something better of me. That's another good part about being an adult. Otherwise, you'd be afraid of your own shadow.

[LLOYD *has returned to the bed, still holding the hammer. He nods, thinking he understands.*]

LLOYD: Well, I wouldn't be a worthy opponent, anyway. My upper body could use more definition.

BERNICE: [*Shrugs.*] As long as it's not concave, it's okay.

LLOYD: If he came at me, I might actually—cower, would that be all right? Though, of course, we never know what we'll do until we—maybe I'd be a man, in the most obvious sense of the—instinctive and animal—tooth and nail, hammer and—

[*Sees hammer in his hand*]

Hey, look at me, I'm halfway home, hammer and—

BERNICE: Would you please knock it off?

[*He stops, chastened, confused.*]

LLOYD: Sorry.

BERNICE: Don't be so antsy.

[*Refers to bed.*]

After that last half-hour? You did a hell of a lot.

LLOYD: So, what *do* you want me to do?

BERNICE: Just sit there and smile at me in your underwear, that's very pleasant. Or if your face gets tired or your can gets cold, or you really have to use that hammer, help me out here. It's your home, after all.

LLOYD: It's both of ours, if you think about it.

[*She does think.*]

BERNICE: In a way. For awhile. Absolutely.

[*She rises, starts to kick into her pants.*]

BERNICE: Come on. You'll need *some* skills. And this is the only thing I know to show you. Before you have to go.

[*She exits. Lights fade. Then, in the dark,* LLOYD *hears two men's voices down in the vestibule—the one who screamed at the window, and another—whispering...*]

OTHER MAN'S VOICE: Shh—give me that—

MAN #2'S VOICE: Would you please be more careful?

OTHER MAN'S VOICE: Who cares? It's supposed to just, like, saturate itself, isn't it?—All over the—

MAN #2'S VOICE: Well, back up with it, for Christsake, like laying a carpet—or, otherwise, we'll be in it ourselves.

OTHER MAN'S VOICE: I see. So it's like painting an apartment.

MAN #2'S VOICE: Exactly.

OTHER MAN'S VOICE: Or filling up one of those old tubs to the top—

MAN #2'S VOICE: Outdoors, like in an old Africa movie—

OTHER MAN'S VOICE: —until it overflows.

MAN #2'S VOICE: Right. Now give me the stick—

OTHER MAN'S VOICE: And slap it on?

MAN #2'S VOICE: Yeah. Like we're painting Frank's fat fucking face.

[*Lights rise, suddenly. Opposite* LLOYD, BERNICE *enters, dressed differently now, more normal. He, too, is more spruced up. And very agitated.*]

BERNICE: What do you mean, calling me up at this hour of the—

LLOYD: This is what I've been trying to tell you.

[*He is taking off his shoes, which are dripping with something.*]

BERNICE: What, that?

LLOYD: Look at my socks, look at my shoes. These are my good shoes, and now they're covered in white sticky paint, like a pair of Dr. Seuss' shoes. But how could I reach the lobby door otherwise? It was like crossing the Red Sea, only it was white, and it didn't separate, it sucked me right in.

BERNICE: You were so cute when you were calm...

LLOYD: After they poured paint into the vestibule, they slapped a final line on your mailbox, they marked Frank like the angel of death does in the Passover tale—only he's not going to be saved, he's going to be sacrificed, anyone can see.

[*All the while, shaking her head at him,* BERNICE *has taken off his shoes, cleaned them.*]

BERNICE: Why were you wearing your good shoes?

LLOYD: What?

BERNICE: Where did you go tonight?

LLOYD: To dinner.

BERNICE: Alone?

LLOYD: What difference does that make?

BERNICE: Well, why didn't she come up with you?

LLOYD: Because apparently I wasn't worth ruining a pair of shoes for! Oh, now you know, well, why not? She was some woman. I mean, what's my responsibility to you, anyway, when I'm just—

BERNICE: Renting space?

[*Beat.*]

LLOYD: All right.

BERNICE: Then why warn me all this time?

LLOYD: Because he's *your* husband, that's why. And like you said, I have to live here.

[BERNICE *turns on him.*]

BERNICE: Well, it's one thing to slap a coat of paint on, it's another to knock down a Goddamn wall!

LLOYD: Oh, I see, thanks for defining your philosophy: get close but only until it becomes uncomfortable.

BERNICE: No, you think being involved means inter-fucking-fering, when in fact it means leaving someone else alone!

LLOYD: Like you and Frank, you mean? Loving him is just lettin' it rip?

BERNICE: This from a man who thought a leaky faucet was a slit wrist!

[*Beat.*]

Nothing is going to happen to him!

LLOYD: That's not what Frank told me.

BERNICE: What?

LLOYD: Well, you know…that's how I took it.

[*She just looks at him.*]

BERNICE: And when did you talk to *him?*

LLOYD: What difference does that make?

BERNICE: You had no right to—for good or for bad, it's my business!

[*Beat.*]

I've done what I can, *okay?*

LLOYD: No. It's not.

[*Beat.* BERNICE *looks up, disgustedly.*]

BERNICE: Jesus. No wonder that college girl couldn't eat. If I were your lover, I'd lose my appetite, too.

LLOYD: Oh? And what have you been?

BERNICE: Your landlord! And you've only got till Friday to pay the fucking rent!

[*Quieted by this…*]

LLOYD: You'll get it. My parents will… whatever.

BERNICE: Well, what else would a little boy do, right?

[*Then—*]

Wherever you go, you create a crisis, so you can solve it, because worrying is your way to stay in control. Well, it may work for you, but it's been driving me fucking crazy!

LLOYD: [*A tough guy.*] And you think love's just a nice long bath. Well, sometimes it's a scalding hot shower, baby!

BERNICE: And that sounds so inviting, doesn't it? I'll pass your number to all my girlfriends.

[*Beat. Then, helplessly, he approaches her, plaintive now.*]

LLOYD: Don't you understand? How can I see—I can't see something bad happen again. What am I supposed to do, just stand by and watch while—

BERNICE: No, you can eat me out more often than my husband does, okay? That's the extent of your obligation. Just be the boyfriend. Just love me a little. Please.

LLOYD: Is that all I'm good for? A last little "palate cleanser" before—

BERNICE: It's not so small a thing to me.

LLOYD: Some kind of final sedative before—

BERNICE: I've tried to make sure it wasn't one-sided.

LLOYD: Oh, and is this the exchange? It's not equal.

[*Beat.*]

BERNICE: Before September, what other commitment can we make?

LLOYD: You said so yourself, it's all a short-term lease.

[*Beat. Caught...*]

BERNICE: Did I say that? Well, next time, don't go looking for lessons on life from your super, okay?

[*Beat. She waits. Then—furiously—*]

BERNICE: Look—it's June first, or it's September—you never arrived, or better yet, you're already out! If you've got the guts to go!

[*Then she leaves, slamming the door behind her. LLOYD stays there. He sits on the bed. Then he lies down, tries to sleep. Lights dim.*]

[*Then—downstairs, door slams, loudly. Baby shrieks. Gunshot.* LLOYD *springs up in bed. He grabs the hammer. Then there is banging on his door. After a second, it flies open.* LLOYD *catches his breath.* FRANK *is in the doorway, panting. He approaches. Then, seeing the hammer... stopping...*]

FRANK: When I got in...they had locked the baby in the bathroom... Then they... they got Bernice and not me... They came at me from the other side, who'd have suspected?... Don't you see? There was nothing I could do, nothing anyone could have done...

[FRANK *just stands there, his chest heaving.*]

[*Then—suddenly—all the improvements in the apartment start to collapse: the cabinet door drops down, the curtain falls off.*]

[LLOYD *sees all this. Hopelessly, he slowly drops the hammer.*]

[*Lights fade.*]

END OF PLAY

WORLD WITHOUT MEMORY

Seth Kramer

Thank you Robin

World Without Memory by Seth Kramer. Copyright © 2002 Seth Kramer. All rights reserved.

CAUTION: Professionals and amateurs are hereby warned that *World Without Memory* by Seth Kramer is subject to a royalty. It is fully protected under the copyright laws of the United States of America, and of all countries covered by the International Copyright Union (including the Dominion of Canada and the rest of the British Commonwealth), and of all countries covered by the Pan-American Copyright Convention and the Universal Copyright Convention, and of all countries with which the United States has reciprocal copyright relations. All rights, including professional, amateur, motion picture, recitation, lecturing, public reading, radio broadcasting, television, video or sound taping, all other forms of mechanical or electronic reproduction, such as information storage and retrieval systems and photo-copyright, and the rights of translation into foreign languages are strictly reserved. Particular emphasis is laid upon the question of readings, permission for which must be secured from the author's agent in writing.

Inquiries concerning all performing rights to the play should be addressed to the author's agent, Ronald Gwiazda, ROSENSTONE/WENDER, 38 East 29th Street, New York, New York 10016.

Seth Kramer

Since moving to New York City eight years ago, **SETH KRAMER** has been honored to receive such playwriting awards as the George R. Kernodle Award, Kennedy Center's Award For Playwriting Excellence, New York Thespian Award, The Iowa Writer's Alliance Prize and a grant from the Peter S. Reed Foundation.

Seth has a collection of seven short plays titled *After the Beep* published by Dramatic Publishing Company and is the founder of Word of Mouth Productions.

CHARACTERS:

ABE, in his 70s, fairly fit for his age
ROBIN, a handsome woman in her 30s
BOB, a chunky balding man in his 40s
BOB-2
VOICE

SCENE 1

[*Lights up.* ROBIN *and* ABE *sit across from each other at a table, a few empty plates between them. There is a pause in conversation.* ROBIN *finishes a bit of food and looks at* ABE *expectantly. A few pregnant beats.*]

ABE: [*Blinking.*] I'm sorry. I'm sorry, I missed that.

ROBIN: You did?

ABE: Yes, I missed that. My attention must have wandered for a moment.

ROBIN: Oh.

ABE: I don't know what happened.

ROBIN: It's ok.

ABE: Please, would you... um...

ROBIN: Sure, all right. Where do you want me to start from?

ABE: [*Beat.*] I don't know. Just go back, go back to the part about...

[*Pause, reaching.*]

ROBIN: The last little bit?

ABE: Sure.

ROBIN: Ok. It's not all that important though.

ABE: Nonsense. Please.

ROBIN: I was just saying that Robby and I are having a hard time deciding what we are going to do next month.

ABE: You're fighting?

ROBIN: You know how he gets.

ABE: I also know how *you* get.

ROBIN: Dad!

ABE: You're stubborn. You're pig-headed half the time.

ROBIN: Oh, you think anyone who disagrees with you is pig-headed.

ABE: You're just like your mother.

ROBIN: Do you want to hear this or not?

ABE: All right, go on. Tell me.

ROBIN: Well, he comes home yesterday and tells me we are going to spend our vacation time visiting his brother up in Vermont.

ABE: So?

ROBIN: He *tells* me. Forget the fact I think his brother is an asshole, ok? Forget that. Also forget the fact we had already discussed this and decided that this year we were going to do something else. Something exciting. Go to Europe or Tahiti or something. Everything we had talked about meant nothing. It's the fact that he had the nerve to *tell me*.

ABE: Fishing.

ROBIN: Dad...

ABE: No, no, no. Fishing. If I've told you one time I've told you two thousand times. There is nothing in this life like waking up before the world with someone you love, packing up a boat, and going out onto a glass still lake to fish the day away.

ROBIN: I know, Dad.

ABE: What could be better than just the two of you alone at the quietest place in the world?

ROBIN: Room service? A manicure? I could give you a list.

ABE: Nonsense. The zing when you cast out. The soft plunk into the water and the ripple it sends out. Then it's—wunk, wunk, wunk—as you reel back in. It's like meditation. Waiting for that first slight tug, that unmistakable kick of life when you finally get one on the line.

[*Beat.*]

But it's the waiting, see? The waiting is what it's all about. Checking your line. Reeling back in. Casting again. The anticipation.

ROBIN: The bugs, the squishy worms, the odor of dying fish.

ABE: I used to take your mother fishing, you know? She never complained like you do. She was twice as good company as any man I've ever fished with because she wasn't a man. She was your mother.

ROBIN: I know Dad.

ABE: Lake Oka-Bodgi.

ROBIN: Lake Oka-Bodgi.

ABE: That's right. We'd fish, drink beer and talk about anything the world cared to offer up—and the sun would creep up so slowly, and if we were lucky, we'd already have half a cooler full of fish. Then at night your mother would clean those fish, I'd build us a fire and cook 'em up something special.

[*Smiles.*]

There is nothing, never has been and never will be, that can taste like those days on lake Oka-Bodgi with your mother. Nothing.

ROBIN: I know Dad.

ABE: You were conceived at Lake Oka-Bodgi, you know. That's all you two need. Fishing. You and Bobby ought to go fishing.

ROBIN: Dad, I still *hate* fishing.

ABE: Hate fishing?

ROBIN: I've always hated fishing. You and mom kept dragging me out to that boring lake until I turned 12 and got covered with leeches. Remember?

ABE: I...

ROBIN: No fishing. And don't you dare mention it to Robert. I mean it. God, what a nightmare that would be, stuck on a boat for two weeks with that man's brother.

ABE: I don't... I don't remember it like that. I don't ...

ROBIN: Dad?

ABE: Your mother loved fishing.

[*Black out.*]

SCENE 2

[*Lights up.* ABE, *dressed in a robe, sits on a couch watching TV, clicking a remote. A pause.* BOB *walks in adjusting his tie. He wears a sharp three-piece suit. He sees* ABE *and stops.*]

BOB: What is this?

ABE: What is what?

BOB: What are you doing here?

ABE: Watching TV. What does it look like?

BOB: I can see that. Why?

ABE: I don't know, the TV was here, I was here. It seemed like a good idea at the time.

BOB: Jesus, Abe, why do you do this to us?

ABE: Do what? If you have something you'd rather watch I'll change the channel.

BOB: Robin! Robin, come in here for a second.

ABE: Tattle-tale.

[ROBIN *enters, putting on earrings.*]

ROBIN: What? I'm late already, I don't have time...

BOB: Look what I found.

ABE: Hi.

ROBIN: What are you doing here?

BOB: Watching TV, of course.

ROBIN: You're not funny.

ABE: You want to watch something?

BOB: I'm not trying to be.

ABE: Are you two feeling all right?

BOB: [*Under breath.*] He forgot.

ROBIN: Dad, what day is it?

ABE: Day?

BOB: Yes, the day, Abe. Tell us the day.

ABE: What the hell type of question is that? You don't think I know what day it is? It's Tuesday.

BOB: Thursday.

ABE: Tuesday-Thursday, when you're retired those two become interchangeable.

ROBIN: Do you know where you're supposed to be right now?

ABE: Watching TV?

ROBIN: Damn it, Dad!

BOB: [*Under breath, sing-songy.*] I'm telling you—he forgot.

ABE: I did not forget!

ROBIN: So you did this on purpose?

ABE: No, of course not! But I didn't forget either.

[*Pause, begrudgingly.*]

Forget what?

BOB: I knew it.

ROBIN: You have an important appointment today.

BOB: Correction, he *had* an important appointment today.

ABE: I did?

ROBIN: The doctor, Dad. You need to go see the doctor so he can run a few tests.

ABE: [*Sour.*] Oh, that.

BOB: This is the second time he's pulled this, you know.

ROBIN: He didn't *pull* anything, Robert.

BOB: The clinic is going to be none too happy.

ABE: I don't like doctors.

ROBIN: He's not doing this on purpose.

ABE: They poke you with needles.

BOB: I wouldn't be too sure.

ABE: Stick things in the "No Entry" porthole.

BOB: His "problem" seems pretty selective, if you ask me.

ABE: Stop doing that! Stop talking about me like I just left the room.

ROBIN: Get dressed, Dad. Robby, go call the clinic, see if they'll let us reschedule for later today.

BOB: They won't.

ROBIN: Just do it.

    [BOB *exits.*]

ABE: I'm not going.

ROBIN: Oh yes you are.

ABE: Oh no I'm not.

ROBIN: Dad, please, stop being difficult. As it is, I'm going to have to take another day off work, which I can't afford, just to chaperone you down to the clinic.

ABE: I don't need a chaperone.

ROBIN: I wish that were true. If I don't take you myself now...

ABE: I'll go if I say I'm going.

ROBIN: You'll end up at the Yankee game and come home all sunburned.

ABE: The Yankees are playing today?

ROBIN: Go get dressed.

ABE: But my programs...

ROBIN: Go!

ABE: [*Gets up, sullen.*] I should have punished you more when you were a child.

[*Defiant.*]

I'm not wearing a tie.

ROBIN: Fine.

ABE: I don't like ties and I don't like hospitals and I'm sure as hell not going to be forced to put on a tie just to go to the hospital!

ROBIN: I said fine.

ABE: Goddamn doctors, Goddamn old age, Goddamn prostates! I better not miss my shows. If that perverted ghoul tries to bend me over and so much as touch me with a rubber glove, they're going to have to do exploratory surgery on him just to find the damn thing. You get me?

[*Defiant.*]

I still got my dignity.

ROBIN: That isn't what you're seeing the doctor about, Dad.

ABE: It isn't?

ROBIN: No. We talked about this already, when I first made the appointment for you.

ABE: You promise?

ROBIN: On Mother's grave. Now, for the last time, go change clothes.

[ABE *begins to exit, stops, turns.*]

ABE: [*Hesitant, nervous.*] Robin, why do I have to go see the doctor?

[*Black out.*]

SCENE 3

[*Lights up to a dim glow.* ABE *lies on an angled table, his eyes wide open and a frightened look on his face. A blanket covers his body. A thin beam of light rolls up and back along his head, face, and neck. A dispassionate* VOICE *speaks over an intercom system. Its tone is one of forced patience.*]

VOICE: Please, Mr. Rothstein. We need you to hold still during this, all right? Can you do that for me? It'll all be over before you know it. Try and relax. A lot of people fall asleep during this. It's really a very simple...

ABE: The light.

VOICE: Yes, why don't you shut your eyes, Mr. Rothstein. Lie back, relax. Pretend that you're taking a nap at home.

ABE: The light.

VOICE: Mr. Rothstein, if you keep moving around none of the information we gather is going to be any good. We need you to *hold still* or we're going to have to redo the entire procedure.

[*Abe brings his hands up to his face.*]

Please, keep your hands at your sides. Mr. Rothstein? We *need* you to keep your hands at your...

[*Beat.*]

Mr. Rothstein?

[*Pause.*]

Can we get someone in there and strap him in? I don't have all day for this. It's going to be all right. Mr. Rothstein? Mr. Rothstein?

ABE: Why am I here?

[*Black out.*]

SCENE 4

[*Lights up. ROBIN and BOB sit on a couch working. A stack of video tapes sits on a table. BOB smokes his pipe. ABE enters and looks around confused.*]

ABE: [*Pause.*] Robin?

ROBIN: [*Not looking up.*] Yeah, Dad?

ABE: What are you doing?

ROBIN: Working.

ABE: On what?

ROBIN: It's just a couple of documents. I have to read up on this company's history, go over some financial reports, mark them up. That sort of thing.

ABE: Oh.

ROBIN: [*Looking up.*] Is something wrong?

ABE: I... No. No.

ROBIN: Do you need something?

ABE: I've lost...

[*Beat.*]

I'm looking for something.

ROBIN: What is it?

ABE: I can't remember.

BOB: [*Exchanging look with* ROBIN.] Is it your medication?

ABE: [*Annoyed.*] No.

ROBIN: Movies?

ABE: Yes. Yes, that's it.

ROBIN: Do you want to return them now?

ABE: I want my movie card.

ROBIN: Your card?

ABE: I want to rent some movies. I thought we could watch something together.

BOB: We're working.

ABE: When you're finished then. Have you seen my card?

ROBIN: Dad, we've already rented a bunch of movies.

ABE: You did?

BOB: [*Under breath.*] Only took about two hours.

ROBIN: They're on the table.

ABE: Oh good, then I'll just watch these. That'll save me a walk. Can I pop one in?

ROBIN: No, Dad... we already...

BOB: Why don't you watch them upstairs, huh, Abe? Like I've already said, we're working.

ABE: Do you want me to wait?

BOB: [*Another significant look*] No. No, that's all right.

ABE: It's no fun watching them alone.

ROBIN: We... um... we've already seen these.

ABE: You have?

BOB: Yes, we watched them earlier, remember?

[ABE *picks up the tapes and stalks off. After he leaves,* BOB *removes his glasses and rubs his eyes.* ROBIN *starts to cry.* BOB *puts his arms around her. Black out.*]

SCENE 5

[*Lights up.* ABE *sits alone in a spotlight. He holds a photograph.*]

ABE: I have this picture.
    I know it's mine because I keep it in my wallet. It's an old black-and-white of me holding a fish. The fish is a pike that runs the length of my entire arm—beautiful and sleek and long. In the picture I'm a lot younger, a chubby face that is beaming from ear to ear. The lake in the background is good old Lake Oka-Bodgi.
    Next to me stands a man in knee-high boots wearing a pair of old fashioned suspender pants. He has a hat tipped back on his head, his hand resting on my shoulder and his face is split by this crooked grin of pride.
    I've looked and looked and looked...

[*Reaching inside.*]

Studied every inch of that picture, I keep expecting to see something in those black-and-white eyes—something I'll know. The way his hand felt, the slant of his smile... but nothing ever comes.

[*Pause.*]

I keep a black-and-white stranger with me at all times in my wallet.

I don't think I'll ever never know his name again.

[*Black out.*]

<u>SCENE 6</u>

[*Lights up,* BOB *and* ROBIN *stand around a table arguing with each other in hushed tones.* ABE *stands in the doorway, out of sight, listening.*]

BOB: Look. Look...

ROBIN: It's not your place to say.

BOB: Look...

ROBIN: I don't want to discuss this.

BOB: You're being stubborn, Robin.

ROBIN: And you're being cruel.

BOB: Hey, I'm not the bad guy here. I'm not trying to manipulate any-one's opinion and I don't want you to say I made you do this...

ROBIN: Fine, then don't.

BOB: Robin...

ROBIN: What?

BOB: Let's be rational.

ROBIN: Don't throw that word at me. Don't think you can hide your sim-ple justifications for... for... what would you have me do?

[*Beat.*]

What would *you* do in my situation?

BOB: What would *I*...

ROBIN: Yes.

BOB: I *am* in your situation. I *am*.

ROBIN: He's my father, Bobby.

BOB: Mine too.

ROBIN: Oh, please.

BOB: Your dad has always been there for us. He helped build this house. Made me feel like his *son*. You think this is easy for me?

ROBIN: He has good days.

BOB: The doctor said...

ROBIN: I know what the doctor said.

BOB: Then you should know it's best for all of us.

ROBIN: *No!* What I know is that it will be *easiest* for us, but not for him. For him it would be a nightmare. I can't believe you're telling me to...

BOB: I'm not *telling* you to do anything.

ROBIN: *I can't.*

BOB: What are we supposed to do then, huh? Do you want to quit your job so you can stay home with him? Take care of him? Give up your career? Because that's what it's going to take.

[*Pause, no answer.*]

Every day he gets worse. You've seen him, he watches the same movies over and over. He asks the same questions. He goes to the store to buy something but doesn't bring any money. Yesterday he started running a bath and then wandered off without a word. Nearly flooded the whole fucking house.

ROBIN: He just makes a few mistakes.

BOB: He needs to be *watched*, Robin. We can't keep taking care of him.

ROBIN: [*Pause.*] He's my father.

BOB: I know. That's why we have to do something.

[ABE *turns and exits. Black out.*]

SCENE 7

[*Lights up*, ABE *stands in a harshly lit section of the stage, cowering next to a pay phone. He looks confused and frightened. Crowd noise can be heard. The sounds of heavy traffic come in. Horns honking. At least one siren should approach and then fade away.*]

ABE: [*Muttering to himself.*] 976... 976... 976-5... something... 976-5... 636.

[*Picks up phone, dials.*]

976-5636... 976-5636... 976... Hello, Robin? Robin? Can I speak to Robin? Please, my name is Abraham Rothstein... I need... No. I made a mistake then. I misdialed. I'm sorry.

[*Hangs up.*]

976... 976-5363... 563... 976...

[*Pause.* ABE *dials the operator.*]

Hello, operator? I am having a problem, I need help. I went for a walk and got lost. Now I... I can't remember my phone number anymore. I can't remember my phone number.

[*Beat.*]

The last name is Rothstein... Yes, that's right R-O-T-H-S-T-E-I-N. Try Robin, that's my daughter's name, she'll be able to come and get me... she'll know what to do.

[*Beat.*]

I don't know. It's a... a tree name, I think. Something... something tree street. 976. I remember those numbers. 976. And then 5 maybe.

[*Becoming frantic.*]

My name is Abraham Rothstein. I have a daughter, her name is Robin. 976... and I have to speak to her so she can come get me. I need help. I need help!

I don't know where I am.

[*Black out.*]

SCENE 8

[*Lights up. ABE sits on a park bench, holding bread crumbs. He smiles blissfully, enjoying a beautiful day. One of his shoes is missing. A pause. BOB-2 enters. BOB-2 should be a DIFFERENT ACTOR wearing the same clothes as BOB. His manners are exactly the same. He is the same person only, since ABE has forgotten him, he is a stranger now. He looks at ABE.*]

BOB-2: Hello.

ABE: Good morning.

BOB-2: Do you mind if I sit down?

ABE: What, here?

BOB-2: Yes.

ABE: All right.

BOB-2: Thank you.

ABE: It's a free country.

BOB-2: Yes, I suppose it is.

ABE: You have to sit fairly still or the pigeons won't come near you.

BOB-2: [*Long pause.*] Nice day.

ABE: Mmmmm.

BOB-2: Plenty of sun.

ABE: Mmm.

BOB-2: How long have you been out here?

ABE: How long?

BOB-2: Yes.

ABE: I... I don't know.

BOB-2: I see.

ABE: A while. I don't know. It was nice out. I was walking, the sun, the quiet. I just sat down and started feeding the birds. My mind must have wandered.

BOB-2: All right.

ABE: I'm not wearing my watch. I must have left my watch somewhere. I don't know what time it is.

BOB-2: It's OK.

[*Beat.*]

Do you know that you're missing one of your shoes?

[ABE *laughs, delighted by this. He wiggles his toes and looks at* BOB-2, *who looks concerned.* ABE *laughs again at his toes.*]

ABE: [*Sighing, content.*] Funny, huh?

BOB-2: Do you know what happened to it?

ABE: [*Furrows brow.*] Nope. I have one, I don't have the other.

[*He chuckles again.*]

Shoes.

BOB-2: [*Pause.*] Do you want to go now?

ABE: Go?

BOB-2: Yes.

ABE: Go where?

BOB-2: Abe, are you feeling all right?

ABE: Of course I feel all right, I've...

[*Suddenly wary.*]

... never... felt... better.

BOB-2: What? What is it?

ABE: How did you know my name?

BOB-2: Know your name?

ABE: Yes, how did you know my name?

BOB-2: Abe, this isn't funny.

ABE: Funny? I had better go.

BOB-2: Wait, wait...

ABE: Don't try and follow me.

BOB-2: Follow you?

ABE: I'll call the police.

BOB-2: Abe, what the hell is going on? It's been hours...

ABE: Hours?

BOB-2: Yeah, almost 12 hours.

ABE: I don't know what you're talking about...

BOB-2: Robin's been worried sick. You disappear without a word. God only knows what could have happened to you. I had to take the afternoon off work to come look for you. I've had enough.

[*Stands.*]

The car is only a few blocks away. Let's go.

ABE: Don't touch me.

BOB-2: Abe, I'm going to take you home.

ABE: I said don't touch me.

BOB-2: You're not drunk are you?

ABE: I don't know who you... who you are...

BOB-2: Robin is going to have a fit if you've been drinking.

ABE: I don't know what you're... I don't...

BOB-2: Abe... come on.

[BOB-2 *takes* ABE's *arm.*]

ABE: Help me! Someone *help me! ! ! I'm being attacked! ! ! Someone help me! ! !*

[*Black out.*]

SCENE 9

[*Lights up.* ABE, *alone in a spot. He is perfectly lucid and peaceful.*]

ABE: A world without memory is a world of the present.

The past exists only in books, in documents. In order to know himself, each person carries his own Book of Life, which is filled with the history of his life. With time, each person's Book of Life thickens until it cannot be read in one sitting. And then comes a choice—accept the burden of time or abandon the past.

Without his Book of Life, a person is a snapshot, a two dimensional image, a ghost. It doesn't matter if yesterday they were rich or poor, educated or ignorant, proud or humble, in love or empty-hearted—no more than it matters how a soft wind gets into their hair. Such people look you directly in the eye and grip your hand firmly. Such people walk with the limber strides of their youth.

For it is only habit and memory that dull our passions. Without memory each night is the first night. Each morning, the first morning, and each kiss stolen for the first time.

In a world without memory.

[*Black out.*]

SCENE 10

[*Lights up.* ABE *sits on a bed in a robe.* ROBIN *sits across from him.*]

ABE: Something is wrong. Something is wrong.

ROBIN: What is it?

ABE: I can't... I don't...

ROBIN: Dad...

ABE: Where are my cigarettes?

ROBIN: You shouldn't smoke, Dad.

ABE: Where are my goddamn cigarettes?

ROBIN: You quit.

ABE: Now listen here...

ROBIN: You quit smoking almost six years ago.

ABE: That's impossible.

ROBIN: Do you remember what your doctor told you? What he said about your lungs?

ABE: I hate doctors.

ROBIN: He said that if you keep smoking the walls of your lungs would become so brittle...

ABE: This is ridiculous.

ROBIN: ... so brittle that you may tear one. That your breathing would become impaired...

ABE: [*Truly confused.*] Why are you doing this?

ROBIN: [*Long pause.*] What?

ABE: Why have you brought me here? Why won't these people let me leave?

ROBIN: Dad...

ABE: Have I done something wrong? Are you punishing me?

ROBIN: This your new home.

ABE: Home.

ROBIN: This is where you live now.

ABE: I want to leave.

ROBIN: No.

ABE: I want to leave with you.

ROBIN: You can't.

ABE: Why?

ROBIN: It's become too difficult. It's better for you here.

[*Beat.*]

I'm sorry Dad.

ABE: I lose things here. They take things away from me. My cigarettes, my watch, my favorite fishing rod. I used to have so much and now I can't find... now it's all gone.

[*Beat.*]

Things are disappearing.

ROBIN: Maybe I should call the doctor.

ABE: *No!* Please, don't. I'm sorry. I didn't mean that. I'll be good. I didn't...

[*Long pause.* ABE *lies down on the bed.* ROBIN *watches.*]

ROBIN: I have to go. I'll come visit you again tomorrow.

ABE: Tomorrow.

ROBIN: That's right. Tomorrow. I'll bring Robby with me, all right?

ABE: Who?

ROBIN: [*Beat.*] A friend. I'm sure you'll like him.

ABE: If you say so.

ROBIN: We'll go for a walk tomorrow, around the pond. Would you like that? Dad?

[*Pause.*]

I'll be back tomorrow.

[*She turns to leave.*]

ABE: Robin?

ROBIN: Yes?

ABE: Tell me about... tell me about... I can't remember how it goes.

ROBIN: The lake?

ABE: [*Beat, very clear.*] Tell me about the lake.

[ROBIN *puts her bag down and sits. Takes* ABE's *hand.*]

ROBIN: [*A gentle tone.*] Lake Oka-Bodgi.

ABE: Lake Oka-Bodgi.

ROBIN: That's right. Waking up before the world with someone you love, packing up a boat, and going out to fish the day away.

ABE: Your mother.

ROBIN: [*Trying to get it just right.*] You'd fish, drink beer and talk about anything the world cared to offer up. The zing when you'd cast out. The soft plunk into the water—the wunk, wunk, wunk—as you reel back in—and at night mother would clean the fish, and you'd build a fire.

ABE: [*Struggling.*] There is nothing... never has... never will... that tastes like those days on Lake... Oka-Bodgi... nothing.

[*Beat, clear.*]

I still remember.

<u>END OF PLAY</u>

THE PAIN OF
PINK EVENINGS

a monologue

Rosemary Moore

The Pain of Pink Evenings by Rosemary Moore. Copyright © 2002 by Rosemary Moore. All rights reserved. Reprinted by permission of the author.

CAUTION: Professionals and amateurs are hereby warned that *The Pain of Pink Evenings* by Rosemary Moore is subject to a royalty. It is fully protected under the copyright laws of the United States of America, and of all countries covered by the International Copyright Union (including the Dominion of Canada and the rest of the British Commonwealth), and of all countries covered by the Pan-American Copyright Convention and the Universal Copyright Convention, and of all countries with which the United States has reciprocal copyright relations. All rights, including professional, amateur, motion picture, recitation, lecturing, public reading, radio broadcasting, television, video or sound taping, all other forms of mechanical or electronic reproduction, such as information storage and retrieval systems and photo-copyright, and the rights of translation into foreign languages are strictly reserved. Particular emphasis is laid upon the question of readings, permission for which must be secured from the author's agent in writing.

All inquiries concerning performance rights should be addressed to Joyce Ketay, Joyce Ketay Agency, 1501 Broadway, Suite 1908, New York, N.Y. 10036.

Rosemary Moore

ROSEMARY MOORE'S most recent production was the New York premiere of *The Pain of Pink Evenings* at HERE, part of "The American Living Room Festival" of 2001, directed by Sonja Moser, performed by Wendy Allegaert. In 2000 she was selected as one of five Emerging Playwrights by the Cherry Lane Alternative Mentor Project for the development and production of *Aunt Pieces*, directed by Michael Sexton, mentored by A.R. Gurney. Rosemary Moore has performed her original monologue shows at downtown venues in New York City. She received her MFA from NYU's Dramatic Writing Program. Her writing has been published in *BOMB* magazine; *The Breast, An Anthology* (Global City Press); "The Waverly Review" and elsewhere. She teaches as a writer-in-residence for Teachers & Writers Collaborative in the NYC public schools and lives in Brooklyn with her husband Joshua Shneider, saxophonist/composer, and her identical twin daughters, Violet and Faye. She is a member of The Dramatists Guild, the playwrighting unit of The New Group and The Writer's Room.

The Pain of Pink Evenings was originally published in *BOMB* magazine under the name "Raindevils."

CHARACTER:

TRACY LUSK, 40s

TIME:

The present

PLACE:

Washington D.C.

[TRACY LUSK *is pacing in her dark, musky living room. She wears "Certainly Red" lipstick and a bit of very pale foundation. Maybe* TRACY *is confiding to the audience or perhaps talking to herself. Either way she is having an epiphany.*]

TRACY: Henry set me free. He really did. Now maybe I can fall in love again. He came to me in a dream... came rowing over in a red scruffy boat. I was on some shore weeding a vegetable garden. I had never seen the boat before, nor the lake, and he was dressed in a suit, which was odd for him. I immediately ran down to the dock and dipped my dirty hands into the water to rinse them off. Three jets roared overhead so we couldn't talk right away. The boat glided closer but it was obvious he wasn't going to be getting out. He rowed forward a little and backward a little, quietly keeping the boat in one place.

"Tracy," he said, "I've come to say good-bye. It's been ten years since I died and you mustn't think of me anymore. I know you're struggling and I want something good for you."

"But Henry, I rely on you."

"I have a plan," he said.

"I don't know what to say Henry."

"I want you to remember one memory. Something you and I did together. Quickly, now think."

"Well, Henry, I don't know."

"Close your eyes."

"Okay." I closed my eyes and lay back in the sun.

"Have you thought of the memory?"

"No, Henry, not yet."

"Well, that's okay. When you do think of the memory, I want you to identify one object from the memory, a shoe, a handbag, a tie I wore and then buy one just like it, or if you have it in our closet at home take it and throw it in the Potomac River and then start a new life, Tracy."

"But Henry, I haven't seen a real man since you died."

I heard the dipping and raising of the oars as I lay on that dock in the sun. The splashing noise of the oars faded. He was gone. Then I woke up to that terrible, glaring sunny day that came right after Valentine's Day. I got up and spent the morning normally. My daughter brought me breakfast. I saw her and her brother off to school and then went to the kitchen to water the plants and sat in the lawn chair under that ultraviolet lamp and thought hard for that memory. I flipped through all the memories. It's not too hard because we, my side of the family, do live in the past. I remembered he took me away to Elkton, Maryland, to get married (there isn't a lot of red tape there), me the sap. We were on the grass in front of Union Station. We had an hour to kill. Taxi cabs circled the park where we sat. "Tracy we're getting on the train in an hour."

"I know Henry."

"How you got me this far I'll never know."

"How you got *me* this far I'll never know."

"Take off your sweater, Tracy."

"I think I'd rather not." I'd never shown anyone anything but my face. I am strange about all of that.

"It's 80 degrees sweetheart. Aren't you roasting?"

"Not really." I said. Then he smiled a smile that took me right in. My hands began unbuttoning my sweater. I looked down at the little pearls zigzagging all over it, then looked at him one more time and I took it off. Underneath I had on a white silk blouse with short sleeves. My arms were white and hairless and in the crook of each arm were veins, delicate turquoise veins. He lifted one of my arms and kissed that place. So I chose from that memory... I chose the pretty white sweater. It was right in the back of my closet in one of those plastic hanging bags stuffed with mothballs. It took me an hour to leave the lawn chair and go up and get it.

When I reached into that closet I felt criminal and I actually kept my foot propped against the door so it wouldn't slam shut. I unzipped the bag for the first time in ten years. Couldn't have done it before. It would have disturbed me. All those paisley, bohemian skirts and my sequined evening dresses screamed of Henry. I looked through them, resisted bringing them all out. I wanted to complete my dream assignment as soon as possible. I lifted the sweater off its wooden hanger and out of the hanging bag with its ivy patterns, lay it on my arm like a prayer shawl, and zipped the bag up.

I had made the bed that morning. I decided to lay the sweater right in the middle of the bed where the mattress dips. I leaned against the wall and stared at it as if it were some radioactive substance. It glowed. I tried it on and felt a pain in my chest and a button fell off of it. I sat at the vanity thinking of Henry. The sweater wouldn't warm anyone up and the white was more gray now. Must have worn it at least six hundred times. I took it off and tacked it to the bulletin board. I paced around the room, my hips leading my hips, wanting to go right out that window and fly to that damn river. You see war everywhere along the Potomac River. Fathers of our country, guns, rifles, flags, flames, white marble monuments and tourists. I chose to go to that place on the Potomac with the monument of the waves and the seagulls because it had no memories for me and I may travel to the other side of the ocean some day. I felt strange. Kept feeling as though I had long, crazy, black hair like a witch. I kept grabbing at my neck but felt nothing but air.

My father watched me. I thought the doorbell was going to ring and he or some other man would come to the door and stop the ritual so I untacked the sweater and looked out the window and caught a glare of the noonday sun. No one was on the street. The coast was clear. But I had no desire to walk so I made up my face and called a yellow cab. I put the sweater in a brown paper sack. I kept thinking of my father, his white and black skunk hair combed smartly out of his face. He always looked at me like I was guilty and like he was expecting some explanation. Tilting his head and screwing up his mouth, he would. The man was a boy until the day I buried him. Is that what a father is? He taught me to imagine what it would have been like if he had met me instead of the mother I never knew. I'd smile at him and flutter inside. Flutter on by. Bye Daddy. Come back girl. Maybe I'd drown him with this sweater. Wanted to get them all off my mind. I guess I was always surprised that you can stop thinking of them and they just come back.

My father raised me on evening talks. When he'd get home from the ropes we'd sit in the living room, which was lit by the sinking sun, and talk 'til it was black outside. He might have even made up a lot of it, but that didn't matter. In fact some of the stories were fantastic. "There was a man Tracy," he'd say. "There was one amazing man who traveled in a wagon train. This was after wagon trains, Tracy. They'd ride the very, very back roads in the Midwest 'cause they were mostly flat and easy for the horses. This man, Tracy, was a real man for he let his hair grow wild and he rose with the sun. He'd set his mirror against a wagon wheel and sit on a wooden stool every morning and shave his black, black, stubble and then he would call out to the rest of the people. '*Rise*,' he would say, for he was the leader. He was a man with a peculiar heart. It didn't open very often but when it did it couldn't close and it would drive him across rivers and through towns. He took routes that made no sense, for you see, his heart opened on things he couldn't see. He possessed an idea of a woman. He'd conjure up a face and draw it and draw it until he'd get it right and burn all the other tries. The people who traveled with him were pale and ghostly faces... they were platefaces." My father always laughed out loud when he said platefaces. He'd say, "Tracy, it must be time for dinner." Then we'd go into our tiny dining room and eat what I'd fixed. I'd light the candles and he'd say, "Oh, the pain of evening, the pain of pink evenings. What would we do without food?" He'd rub his ribs and arch his back. After we'd eaten he'd light his cigarette and lean back in his chair and stare out the window and resume the wagon train story. He'd tilt so far back in the chair that I always thought it would slip out from under him, but it never did. He'd look out the window which was behind my head. I was a timid girl. I just sat there folding and unfolding and refolding my napkin. Even though he wasn't looking at me I made gasps and giggles and oohs and aaahs. He needed an audience. "You can't imagine, Tracy, how this man traveled once he'd drawn his perfect drawing. He'd park the wagon train outside of each town and make the people stay while he went into the restaurants, shops and movie theaters. Into every neighborhood he'd walk and walk. This man wouldn't stop. This ideal woman tore at him. She put holes in his hands, she bit at his feet, my girl, you've never seen such pain. He felt heart pain as physical pain and if he hadn't found her by sunset he'd go back to the wagon train where the platefaces by this time had prepared dinner for him. They all sat in a circle and ate. No one would mention the search. '*People!*, she's out there. I can feel her,' he screamed. 'Wait!!! I can feel her hot breath on my neck. This time I can even smell her. I'm going back.' This man would walk into town on his long, strong legs. He had reached the age of 44. Hadn't found her. One dark night in the middle of sum-

mer our hero was making his night's return to the outskirts of the
town of Palomino. The moon was full. You can't imagine the pain,
my little Tracy... a kind of supreme being lodged in his chest just
bursting. He walked along the cornfield. Two miles... three miles.
Not one car had come by. Then, out of the darkness he heard the
ribbony, scarlet laugh of a woman and the cry of a baby and then
the low honk of a car. He walked the asphalt, the black, black
asphalt. Up ahead he saw the taillights of a car. He started to run
and run and run and as he approached the car he heard the laugh
again. He could feel the pain melting like a dagger of ice. Next to
a 1952 Chevy sedan stood a woman. She was wearing white shorts
and a white sleeveless shirt. She carried a baby on her hip. 'Excuse
me,' said the man.

The woman turned around. He had found her. She smiled and
said, 'How do you do?'

They leaned against the warm car. Our man lifted the baby up to
heaven and then put it in the car on a pile of blankets. After 44 years
of life and 25 years of search and danger, he'd found her. Lots of
danger. For he was an expert robber, Tracy, my Tracy, for how else
could he support a wagon train? So now he took her in his arms and
said. 'Darling, I've found you and do you have a name?' The mild
summer night filled them. The corn was tiny but filled with spring
lushness. The moon shone down and made the brown soil silver.
'Do you have a name?' The heat of the day seeped up from the black
road. He could now continue his life, let the platefaces go and move
into a house and a farm and be with his 'Who?'

She was a lovely woman. Black hair, long, long, blue-black hair
and long shy eyelashes. She laughed again and pressed her body
against his strong chest and said 'Who are you? Can I be with you?
Can I stay? I could never leave you.'

'Yes, my darling.' he said. This huge, pained man relaxed for the
first time in 44 years. He reached into his shirt pocket and found the
folded up drawing. 'Look,' he said. 'Here you are. I have had to
throw others away because they wouldn't present themselves.' She
gasped and laughed. 'Who are you?' she said.

'I am Walter J. Pim,' he said, wanting her, needing her and in a
whisper said, 'Who are you?'"

By this time my father's eyes would be filled with tears. His hand
would be stretched out like a Biblical man. "'Who are you, my lovely woman?' He lifted her chin up and kissed her. 'Your name is...' She
put her white soft hand into his and finished his sentence. 'Is Tracy.'"

That story always hooked me. By the time he finished the story I would have torn the napkin to shreds and couldn't look into my own father's eyes. But I'd hug my daddy and clear the dishes away.

* * *

I jumped and realized the cab had honked. I put on my trench-coat, grabbed my purse and the little brown sack and got into that yellow cab. I told the cabdriver to go to Lady Bird Johnson Park. I felt like I was going away on a long trip. That day nothing looked bad to me. Even the floor of the cab looked wonderful. A pretty, pink lipstick-stained cigarette butt lay on the floor. The sweater sat in my lap, in the sack like a little cat. I stuck my hand inside it and felt the little pearls and buttons and button holes. The only place a cab could stop was a pull-off resting area on the wrong side of the parkway. Oh well. Shit. I felt good enough to run across. I looked like a bum running across the median strip carrying a paper bag. I love median strips. They remind me of the pitcher's mound. And so there I was at three in the afternoon in the middle of February about ready to throw the sweater into the Potomac River. First though, I lay on the grass to see if I could contact Henry. The sun-light went right through my lids and my clothes. I concentrated so hard you wouldn't believe it. He was nowhere to be found. Then I saw the shadow. My sun was being blocked and I heard voices and footsteps and a foreign language. I opened my eyes. A Japanese man stared down at me as though I were the grave of a famous per-son whose epitaph he had to read. "Excuse me," he said with a thick accent. His face was a skinny triangle with dark eyes and a thin kind smile. I sat up and clutched the bag. I looked over to see several Japanese women clustered under a tree. He motioned to me to go over to them. Oh, I thought... he wants me to take his picture. I didn't really like the disturbance from the ritual but you never know how you are going to be visited. Yes. They must be his wife and daughters. Pretty soon we were all under the tree. Before I could talk, smile, or react, one daughter had pulled me into the sun and the rest followed her and began taking my picture. I took off my sunglasses, told them to wait a second and edged my way over to the monument to sit on the curved peak of one of the lower waves. I might as well give them a good picture. By the time I had gotten comfortable they had all disappeared. I stood up and my sunglasses fell to the cement and cracked. What did this mean? Oh well, I thought and picked up the broken glasses and walked to the edge of the river bank, ripped the paper sack apart, and tossed the sweater out as far as I could.

I watched it float away. It didn't sink, just then. It lay on top of the water like foam. It got caught on some river debris. I thought I'd have to leave it there, hanging on the dead branch. I hopped along the shore until I was even with it and began throwing rocks. It looked sort of sad flailing around and it hurt me to watch it. That poor little girl. The torso finally sank, leaving the two arms begging the sky. Then they went one by one. I watched until it could have been just another glint on the water.

END OF PLAY

WHAT HE SENT

Photos from Brooklyn

Julie Marie Myatt

What He Sent by Julie Marie Myatt. Copyright © 2001 by Julie Marie Myatt. All rights reserved. Reprinted by permission of the author.

CAUTION: Professionals and amateurs are hereby warned that *What He Sent* by Julie Marie Myatt is subject to a royalty. It is fully protected under the copyright laws of the United States of America, and of all countries covered by the International Copyright Union (including the Dominion of Canada and the rest of the British Commonwealth), and of all countries covered by the Pan-American Copyright Convention and the Universal Copyright Convention, and of all countries with which the United States has reciprocal copyright relations. All rights, including professional, amateur, motion picture, recitation, lecturing, public reading, radio broadcasting, television, video or sound taping, all other forms of mechanical or electronic reproduction, such as information storage and retrieval systems and photo-copyright, and the rights of translation into foreign languages are strictly reserved. Particular emphasis is laid upon the question of readings, permission for which must be secured from the author or her agent in writing.

All inquiries concerning performance rights should be addressed to Julie Marie Myatt, c/o Applause Theatre & Cinema Books, 151 West 46th Street, 8th Floor, New York, N.Y. 10036.

Julie Marie Myatt

JULIE MARIE MYATT has had plays produced in New York, Los Angeles, Minneapolis, and Actors Theatre of Louisville. Her ten-minute play *Lift and Bang* is published in *30 Ten-Minute Plays by 2 Actors from Actors Theatre of Louisville* by Smith & Kraus. She received a Walt Disney Studios Screenwriting Fellowship in 1992–93, a Jerome Fellowship at the Playwrights' Center in 1999–2000, and a McKnight Advancement Grant in 2001–2002. Her other plays include *The Pink Factor*, *Cowbird*, *August is a thin girl*, *The Sex Habits of American Women*, *Alice in the Badlands*, and *49 Steps to the Sun*.

CHARACTER:

BILLY

[BILLY *sets up his photo equipment; lenses, flash, tripod, etc. He's obviously a successful photographer. His black and white* SLIDES *show the photos of his evolving new life in Brooklyn, NY.*]

[SLIDE: *A blurry shot of New York.*]

BILLY: June 1998. If I can make it here, I'll make it anywhere. (The "it" remains shaky. But the "I" arrives hopeful.)

[SLIDE: BILLY *stands posing calmly for his own camera. A brownstone behind him.*]

BILLY: My house. Not my house really, but my room. Upstairs. Four floors up. My bed, my books, my cameras. I know none of my neighbors. But I think they like me. I baked cookies and left them on their doorsteps. Have heard nothing yet, but know that's gotta be a shoo-in. I burnt most of them, but given the fact I was using a toaster oven, that's to be expected.

[SLIDE: BILLY *smokes a cigarette. Looking pensive.*]

BILLY: July. I have taken up smoking.

[SLIDE: *A bottle of Jack Daniels.*]

BILLY: I don't like to smoke alone.

[SLIDE: BILLY *stands naked.*]

BILLY: August. I've given up clothes. My neighbors remain distant. I remain optimistic. Sweaty, but steadfast.

[SLIDE: BILLY *in front of subway.*]

BILLY: It takes me thirty minutes to get to work. Forty if I have to wait for the next train. I am working on not staring at people. (I've recently discovered that some people don't appreciate that here. Keep being asked "what the fuck you staring at, asshole?" Needless to say, it came to my surprise that *I* was the asshole.) Still, I want to stare. There's just so many people to watch. So many kinds of faces. Kinds of hair.

[SLIDE: BILLY *with longer hair.*]

BILLY: October. I'm growing my hair. Someone at work asked if I was growing a wig. (Was that supposed to be funny?)

[SLIDE: BILLY *sitting in lively coffee shop.*]

BILLY: I haven't slept in days. (See, this really is the city that never sleeps!) I think I may be drinking too much coffee, but who knows. I think I need sex. More than anything. I think I'm just horny. It keeps me up. Thinking. Wish you were here. For old times sake. I think about that. (Will refrain from asking, "Do you?")

[SLIDE: BILLY *standing in the middle of the Brooklyn bridge.*]

BILLY: December. Don't worry. I'm not thinking of jumping. (Not yet.) But am contemplating, "Have I come to the bridge?" "When to cross it?" Etc.

[SLIDE: BILLY *in crowd.*]

BILLY: I'm lonely.

[SLIDE: BILLY *wearing paper 1999 glasses on his eyes.*]

BILLY: Happy New Year.

[SLIDE: BILLY *in Prospect Park.*]

BILLY: January. I've begun coming here. Lots of dogs. Lots of girls with dogs. Too many of them in couples with dogs. Unfortunately. Lots of dog shit. I watched this greyhound try and hump a poodle the other day. The poodle looked like an indignant cheerleader (as did the owner). The greyhound looked like a starving artist (as did his owner). I suppose their kids would be resigned to marching band or the drill team. Something that allows them to wear tube socks without fear.

(Obviously, the odd mixing of their genes will never allow them to be cool in school. On the upside, weight will never be a problem.) I think I have too much time on my hands. Maybe I need a dog. Pugs are cute. I quit my job. Who needs another damn bookseller. Not I.

[SLIDE: BILLY *in front of theater that boasts an Irish playwright.*]

BILLY: I've never been to Ireland, but I told them Texans like to drink too. I got the job. Painting scenery. I hear the playwright is very hot these days. I don't understand a word he says. I don't think anyone else does either. But it all sounds very cathartic and theatrical. (I'm sneaking dirty pictures into the mist and the moors.)

[SLIDE: BILLY *eating a hot dog.*]

BILLY: March. I've given up vegetarianism and taken up bi-products.

[SLIDE: BILLY *with NY Yankees hat.*]

BILLY: I must find a girl soon. Very soon. I'm hoping I can blend in with the locals. I think Texans get a bad rap. I want to tell them, "Mess with Texas! Mess with Texas! For God's sake, Mess with Texas!"

[SLIDE: BILLY *in bed.*]

BILLY: April. Would you consider a visit?

[SLIDE: BILLY *hand in hand with a woman.*]

BILLY: May. Don't come visit. I've found her.

[SLIDE: *Woman smiling.*]

BILLY: She's from here. She's never left. She never wants to leave.

[SLIDE: *Woman naked.*]

BILLY: I think I'm in love.

[SLIDE: BILLY *alone in a bar.*]

BILLY: She went back to her boyfriend and their dog. (Should have known. They have a Golden Retriever, for Christ's sake. Might as well be Mormons!) She was clingy anyway.

[SLIDE: BILLY *in front of statue of woman.*]

BILLY: I miss Judy. (Her name was Judy. Should have known.)

[SLIDE: BILLY *in front of professional photo shop.*]

BILLY: June. The theater fired me. Discovered that certain hills and vegetables had taken on pornographic shapes during what should have been long, meaningful alcoholic monologues on family violence and the potato famine. But... I finally got the first job I wanted.

[SLIDE: BILLY *in front of different brownstone.*]

BILLY: Here's my new address. I now have room for my bed *and* a chair!

[SLIDE: *Close-up on* BILLY's *face.*]

BILLY: Do I look older to you? I just had another birthday. (You could have remembered.) But. Not bad for 87.

[SLIDE: BILLY *on a street corner.*]

BILLY: July. I'm beginning to feel at home. Someone asked me for directions, and I knew what to tell him. (I later realized it was possibly the opposite way, but it was in the right neighborhood. I'm sure he figured it out.)

[SLIDE: BILLY *sitting opposite a different woman.*]

BILLY: Carmen. Sassy girl. I've met my match. When I asked her to come home with me, she told me I should consider a breath mint first. A one night stand second.

[SLIDE: *Carmen looking pensive in a window.*]

BILLY: When I asked her to pose for me, she laughed. (Apparently photographers don't get the esteem here that they used to.) But, for 50 bucks she relented.

[SLIDE: *Carmen nude on the bed.*]

BILLY: If you can't find love, buy it.

[SLIDE: *Carmen sitting in a chair, her bare back to the camera.*]

BILLY: I think she's warming up to me.

[SLIDE: *Carmen laughing.*]

BILLY: We're getting married.

[SLIDE: BILLY *and Carmen in front of small local church.*]

BILLY: Wish you could have been here. Uh, a little smaller affair than we had? (Live and learn. As you say. Six bridesmaids, seven groomsmen, four parents, and 200 people for a sit-down steak and potato dinner did not a successful marriage make.)

[SLIDE: BILLY *in small kitchen.*]

BILLY: I've moved into Carmen's place. Bigger. (She's got an extra closet where I can set up my equipment.) Life is good.

[SLIDE: *Street corner: market with flowers, fruit.*]

BILLY: You would love this neighborhood. Everything a person needs is here. (OK, maybe a horse would be hard to come by, but really, is that a genuine necessity in this day and age?)

[SLIDE: BILLY *in front of tiny Soho gallery.*]

BILLY: My first show. Wish me luck.

[SLIDE: BILLY *mingling with other artists.*]

BILLY: I sold seven photos for a pretty good sum. Four of them were of Carmen. The other three were cityscapes. (The self-portraits were not among the favorites. Who cares about a hairy guy from Texas?)

[SLIDE: BILLY *with shorter hair.*]

BILLY: I cut my hair. (Actually, Carmen cut my hair. I was asleep at the time.)

[SLIDE: BILLY *smoking in bed.*]

BILLY: January 2000. I gave up smoking for the millennium. Fear of Y2K sent me back to two packs a day. (There's always next year.)

[SLIDE: BILLY *and Carmen in park.*]

BILLY: Carmen thinks pugs are ugly. We got a cat instead. Gary. He jumps around a lot. I think he may be retarded. But he is sweet when he's still.

[SLIDE: *Cat Gary in a bowl.*]

BILLY: He's all mixed up!

[SLIDE: BILLY *in front of a bigger gallery.*]

BILLY: April. Can you come?

[SLIDE: BILLY *at work with photos.*]

BILLY: Wish you could have come to the show. It was a big success. (If I do say so myself.) Sold lots of work. (Even pictures of me. They were blurry, I was naked, and most the buyers were gay, but the shorter hair was key!) I bought two new cameras with my booty. Very exciting. Carmen got a raise at work. We are living high on the hog. (Granted, New York hogs are not near as fat as Texas hogs, but you get the picture.)

[SLIDE: *Carmen standing in dress by window.*]

BILLY: November. Sorry I've been out of touch.

[SLIDE: *Carmen's dress on a hanger.*]

BILLY: Carmen went to Paris for two months. Said she needed space. Haven't slept since. (Do I smother all my wives?)

[SLIDE: BILLY *with Carmen in front of a Christmas tree.*]

BILLY: She came to her senses! (Thank God.) Realizing I remain unmatched in looks, tenderness, and charm. (You never realized this, but I don't hold it against you. Obviously you didn't have the patience for such a poignant discovery.)

[SLIDE: *Poster of George W. Bush glued to a trash can. Someone has given him buck teeth.*]

BILLY: 2001. No matter how much 'splaining I do, seems the entire city has decided I am responsible for the plague that is this new so-called president. Simply because I was birthed in the Long Horn State. Simply because I have an accent (and I am working on that, believe you me), and occasionally wear my blue jeans a tad tighter than the locals, I have become the ridicule of my peers and most strangers. It's become a little too much to bear. Hell, I *too* believe the guy belongs behind a Wendy's counter, not behind the big red button that controls the entire free world. Good God! Lord help us! Four years of the stupidest man to walk the earth. Again, I am forced to repeat, and it's very important this time, "Mess with Texas!"

[SLIDE: *A picture of Brooklyn.* BILLY's *own show.*]

BILLY: My first one-man gig. (Sans the drum, accordion, harmonica get-up.)

[SLIDE: BILLY *with his arm around a tall, smiling woman.*]

BILLY: *So* so glad you could make the show. It meant the world. Carmen was a little put out. (I didn't tell her you were pretty!) But said she really liked you anyway. My friend Doug asked about you. (The drunk guy?) I told him you were still single. He may call you. Rumor has it he's good in the sack. In between blackouts. Sorry about Gary. I will replace those shoes. Size 7? One of these days he'll discover his litter box. It will be Nirvana for us all.

[SLIDE: BILLY *in front of different apartment.*]

BILLY: Our friends moved to Chicago and gave us their apartment. Great location. Great neighbors. Bigger space. We needed more space. Carmen said she'd shoot me if we didn't get a bigger apartment. (I am a Texan, for Christ's sake. To be fair, we are expansive people.)

[SLIDE: *A studio.*]

BILLY: I've found heaven.

[SLIDE: *Close-up on* BILLY.]

BILLY: I have eighteen, no, nineteen gray hairs. I'm thinking of plucking them but nineteen less hairs on my head would be one step closer to my certain fast and impending baldness. I may start wearing hats. Berets are out. (I mean, really. Another photographer with a beret is like too many days with sunshine... glaring down on you in the hottest part of the Sahara Desert... with nothing but a cocktail umbrella to shade you. Torture. Of the worst kind. The ultimate in aesthetic torture—the cliche!) Stocking caps induce a small form of fear and panic in most people. Baseball hats, as I've proved, just make me look all the more redneck. (As someone kindly told me on the street one day, right after he asked me if I had a tail.) Cowboy hat? (About as out as the beret. Might as well wear a Bush/Cheney bumper sticker on my ass.) Perhaps I will bring back the bonnet.

[SLIDE: *A hardback book of* BILLY's *photos.*]

BILLY: This really came out of the blue. (Thank God for "the blue!") Publishers that saw my last show called me and asked me what I had. "Any themes?" I said yeah. A few: Poverty. Loss. Love. Hunger. Alcoholic tendencies. Lung cancer. Houston nightmares. Puerto Rican wife. Impotence. Fear of living. Cat turds. Successful ex-wife. Failure. Myself. Marijuana mornings. Professional doobie rolling. The profound effects of the combination of the harmonica and acoustic guitar on all depths of the soul. Fear of death. Baptist parents. Sin. Sin. Sin. Sin. Sin. My bathroom. Sex. Hair balls. Brooklyn. Girlie pictures. Sin. Sin. Sin. (Guess which one they picked? I was really pushing for the cat turds, but apparently they aren't big coffee table sellers.)

[SLIDE: *Carmen in the kitchen, looking inside the oven.*]

BILLY: What's that? A bun? (Did I mention we're pregnant?)

[SLIDE: *Carmen looking ill.*]

BILLY: Carrying my child seems to be taking its toll. Remember my mother always said she thought she was possessed when she was pregnant with me? I passed this news on to Carmen and she was not amused. She complains that I am too self-involved. (Sound familiar?) Reminds me that she is carrying *her* child as well. Who could only be a saint or an angel. (I sniffed at that, of course.) This unknown creature arrives in August. (If Carmen survives its wrath.)

[SLIDE: *Flowers.*]

BILLY: May. I'm sorry. I wasn't thinking. Really. I should have been more sensitive. Really... but in the end, Sarah, wasn't that a blessing? (Your words.) We already knew then we were doomed together. Didn't we?

[SLIDE: BILLY *posing with other artists.*]

BILLY: Very exciting show coming up. Thrilled to be included with these guys and gals. Should be quite an event. The biggest I've known. I'm nervous. Suddenly all my work looks like I shot it in first grade. During recess. And I'm going to be showing with the high schoolers! Shit! I'm too small for the big time! (Hey, your beautiful flowers arrived. Carmen really appreciated them. As did I.)

[SLIDE: *Carmen's naked round belly.*]

BILLY: Full Moon Rising.

[SLIDE: BILLY *standing on the Brooklyn side of the Brooklyn Bridge.*]

BILLY: Home. (I guess I've come to it.)

[BILLY *is ready to shoot. He sets the timer. Walks in front of the audience and turns toward the camera.*]

[*The camera clicks; there's a flash, captures a photo of* BILLY *standing in front of the audience.*]

BILLY: July 2001...

END OF PLAY

TRAIN STORY

Adam Rapp

Train Story by Adam Rapp. Copyright © by Adam Rapp, 2002. Reprinted by permission of The Joyce Ketay Agency.

CAUTION: All rights reserved. Except for brief passages quoted in newspaper, magazine, radio or television reviews, no part of this book may be reproduced in any form or by any means, electronic or mechanical, including photo opying or recording, or by an information storage and retrieval system, without permission in writing from the Author.

Professionals and amateurs are hereby warned that this material, being fully protected under the Copyright Laws of the United States of America and all other countries of the Berne and Universal Copyright Conventions, is subject to a royalty. All rights including, but not limited to, professional, amateur, recording, motion picture, recitation, lecturing, public reading, radio and television broadcasting, and the rights of translation into foreign languages are expressly reserved. Particular emphasis is placed on the question of reading and all uses of this play by educational institutions, permission for which must be secured from the Author's agent: Carl Mulert, The Joyce Ketay Agency, 1501 Broadway, Suite 1908, New York, New York 10036, (212) 354-6825.

Adam Rapp

A graduate of Clarke College in Dubuque, Iowa, **ADAM RAPP** also completed a two-year fellowship at Juilliard where his play *Dreams of the Salthorse* was produced. His other plays include *Nocturne, Animals and Plants, Blackbird, Faster, Trueblinka, Ghosts in the Cottonwoods*, and *Finer Noble Gases*. Mr. Rapp has been the recipient of the Herbert & Patricia Brodkin Scholarship; two Lincoln Center le Compte du Nouy Awards; a fellowship to the Camargo Foundation in Cassis, France; the 1999 Princess Grace Award for Playwrighting; a 2000 Suite Residency with Mabou Mines; a 2000 Roger L. Stevens Award from the Kennedy Center Fund for New American Plays; and the 2001 Helen Merrill Award for Emerging Playwrights.

Originally a fiction writer, Mr. Rapp is also the author of five novels: *Missing the Piano* (Viking/HarperCollins), *The Buffalo Tree* (Front Street /HarperCollins), *The Copper Elephant* (Front Street/HarperCollins), *Little Chicago* (Front Street), and the forthcoming *33 Snowfish* (Candlewick Press).

CHARACTERS:

WOMAN
GIRL

[*A* WOMAN *speaks to the audience in a cone of light.*]

WOMAN: A cross-country train. New York to Los Angeles. The seventh, eighth hour. I've been line editing yet another first novel about a young man's coming of age. This one happens to be set at a prestigious Eastern prep school. I'm supposed to be on vacation but there are deadlines. I will go to Santa Monica to visit a friend. A man I'd met at a sales conference. His name is Howard. Howard Slutes. We hardly know each other. He is tall and he has a mustache. I would say he is woodsy-looking. The kind of man you might find sitting around a campfire. At a reception following the announcement of the spring list we learn that we share a passion for Graham Greene. His eyes are warm and fatherly. For three days we will walk along the Pacific Coast Highway and watch the lavender sun sink into the ocean. My eyes are raw with fatigue. Clumsy prose and dangling prepositions. I can feel the heat steaming out of them.

[*Another cone of light slowly reveals a* GIRL.]

WOMAN: At a stop somewhere in the Midwest the doors part and let in the smell of oil refineries. The stench somehow venereal. Like whores on the subway. A young girl enters from the adjacent car. She might be eighteen, nineteen. She holds a paper bag containing a forty-ounce bottle of beer. She has eyes like bullet holes. Nothing but pupil. She starts asking around for drugs.

GIRL: Yo, anybody sellin'? I'll take anything. I'll take motherfuckin' Actifed!

WOMAN: It's not for her, she says, it's for her baby.

GIRL: It ain't for me, it's for my baby.

WOMAN: There are maybe seven passengers in my car. They're all either old or sleeping. The girl keeps blowing her nose into her naked hand. I want to ask where her baby is but I'm terrified of what her answer might be. She senses my curiosity the way stray dogs smell fear on you. She turns to me. Morris did it to her, she says. He put that snakebite in her belly.

GIRL: Morris did it to me. He put that snakebite in my belly.

WOMAN: A white girl talking ghetto. Why does this make me feel uncomfortable? Her skin is so pale I think of orchids. Dirty, white orchids. How they go purple at the edges. Her hair is dulled from sorrow more than anything chemical. She calls out to Morris.

GIRL: Yo, Morris, you hidin' in here?!

WOMAN: She is drunk and she talks to everyone.

GIRL: Anybody seen a tall lanky nigga?! Big long bullet head?! Tattoo on his hand?! Two-tone kicks?!

WOMAN: She is small the way adolescent boys are small. She looks to be maybe three or four months pregnant. Despite the dead black winter fields framed in the train window, she wears only a nylon jogging suit. Her nose is gluey, her chin damp. She asks for drugs again.

GIRL: Yo! Do-any-body-got-any-drugs?

WOMAN: She waits. The train moves along with a kind of dumb, affectless inevitability. She suddenly screams that she has a knife and that she's going to cut somebody.

GIRL: I got a knife, people! I'll motherfuckin' cut somebody!

WOMAN: She produces a small nail file. Though a homicide is highly unlikely, the air is suddenly thick. The conductor appears through the hydraulic doors. He tackles her in a very impressive three-part move. He has enormous forearms. There are secret athletes everywhere. His hat falls off. The girl flails. The conductor has to sit on her arms. He literally sits on her arms. Her forty ounces of Old English Eight Hundred are now an amber stream flowing under the seats. The girl cries the way children cry when they fall at the ice rink. Legs splayed. Head lifted defiantly. Desperate UFO eyes. Her nose is bleeding. So much it's as if her face is menstruating. The conductor collects his hat and informs her that at the next stop she will be escorted off the train by the police.

He confiscates her forty-ounce bottle of beer and her nail file. To the seat across the aisle from mine he secures her wrist with a plastic cinch. When he is finished he watches her blankly for a moment. Almost remorsefully. He corrects his hat.

Are you okay? he asks. I didn't mean to hurt you.

Fuck you! she says. Leave me the fuck alone, White Devil!

GIRL: Leave me the fuck alone, White Devil!

WOMAN: She spits at him.

[GIRL *spits.*]

WOMAN: It lands on his hand. The conductor wipes it onto his slacks, and then begins speaking into a walkie-talkie while exiting into the next car. Through my peripheral vision I can see that the girl's nose is still bleeding. I offer her my silk scarf. It's an expensive scarf, Hermes I think, but I don't mind. After all, it's the holiday season. She takes it and stares at it appraisingly. For a moment I think she might stuff it in her pocket, but she balls it up and presses it into her face.

I say, It's silk but don't worry about it. Are you okay?

GIRL: Three hours I waited for that nigga. Three motherfuckin' hours!

WOMAN: Who were you waiting for?

GIRL: Morris.

WOMAN: Is that your boyfriend?

GIRL: Yeah, fuckin' crackhead.

WOMAN: Is he the…

GIRL: The what.

WOMAN: Well, the father.

GIRL: Yeah, that nigga the father. He was s'posed to meet me on the train. You got a square?

WOMAN: A square?

GIRL: Yeah, lady, a square. A cigarette.

WOMAN: I'm sorry, but I don't smoke.
    She shouts to people on the train.

GIRL: Yo, anybody got a cigarette on this train?!…

WOMAN: The old couple behind me appears to be paralyzed with so much fear you'd think a lion was roaming the aisle.

GIRL: Non-smokin' motherfuckers!

WOMAN: She has that kind of wiry strength that comes from survival. You can see it in her hands. How the veins rise up. I ask her her name. What's your name?

GIRL: Why?

WOMAN: Just curious.

GIRL: Exley.

WOMAN: Exley?

GIRL: Yeah, Exley. Is that like funny to you?

WOMAN: No, it's just strange. It happens to be the last name of a well-known novelist. A very promising, but ultimately disappointing well-known novelist. Frederick was his first name. Frederick Exley. Have you heard of him?

GIRL: No.

WOMAN: Do you read?

GIRL: Do I read?

WOMAN: Yes, read.

GIRL: Like *can* I read?

WOMAN: Do you make it a habit?

GIRL: I like read the newspaper. TV Guide and whatnot.

WOMAN: But you don't read literature.

GIRL: Why, you drive the bookmobile or some shit?

WOMAN: I'm an editor.

GIRL: Oh, you like a anchorwoman and shit. You doin' a editorial.

WOMAN: I'm a book editor. My name is Lori.

GIRL: Yeah?

WOMAN: Yeah. Lori Lansky.

GIRL: Cool…Yo, Lori Lansky, you got any pain relief?

WOMAN: I have aspirin.

GIRL: Can I get some?

WOMAN: Sure.
   I reach into my purse and remove a small bottle of aspirin. I unscrew the top and hand her a few. While she's swallowing them, I realize that it's not her nose that's bleeding.
   Are you okay?

GIRL: Why?

WOMAN: Well, it looks like you're losing some blood.

GIRL: You ain't never seen blood before?

WOMAN: Is that coming from your…vagina, Exley?

GIRL: Yeah. That shit won't stop neither.

WOMAN: Did you—are you having a miscarriage?

GIRL: No…Yo, I'm gonna kill that punk-ass nigga.

WOMAN: Morris?

GIRL: Yeah, Morris.

WOMAN: Did he do something to you?

GIRL: *He* didn't do shit.

WOMAN: Did someone else do something to you?

GIRL: Whatchu think?

WOMAN: Exley, if you're having trouble…

GIRL: If I'm having trouble what—you gonna help me?

WOMAN: Well, I think you should tell the conductor so that when the authorities get here they can take you to the hospital. You're losing an awful lot of blood.

GIRL: I ain't goin' to no hospital.

WOMAN: It could be serious.

GIRL: [*Sarcastic.*] For real?

WOMAN: Yes. For real. You may be hemorrhaging.

GIRL: Yo, mind your business, Lori.

WOMAN: We are quiet. I mind my business. Out the window, the black fields have turned white. Somewhere along the way it has started to snow. Silently. Invisibly. The sun has fallen so fast it's as if the earth has slid on its axis. I notice that the manuscript I've been working on is marked up with a kind of brutality. An editorial ruthlessness. The margins are bulging with criticisms. The green ink seemingly carved into the paper. Why did I buy this book?

I look over and notice that Exley's lap is completely red now. Absurdly so. Like something from a horror movie.

GIRL: Yeah, go ahead and judge me, lady.

WOMAN: I say, I'm not judging you.

I am thinking, Don't judge her, Lori. Don't you dare judge her.

GIRL: You think God's gonna get me, don't you, Linda?

WOMAN: Lori.

GIRL: You think God's gonna get me, don't you, Lori?

WOMAN: I wasn't thinking that at all.

GIRL: Yes you was. I can tell. Like that nigga really gives a fuck. He too busy helpin' all the rich people.

WOMAN: I don't think God operates like that.

GIRL: *Operates.* Oh, he a surgeon now?

WOMAN: I don't think he discriminates according to economic stature. He'd be too dependent on the IRS. I think he exercises far more sub-tlety...I'm not judging you, Exley.

She looks at me with a kind of hunger. The way animals beg for food with their eyes. With this look I realize that she's much younger than I thought. Her skin is too fragile. Her cheeks too soft. She may be fifteen, sixteen. For some reason, I ask her if she believes in God.

Do you believe in God, Exley?

GIRL: Why?

WOMAN: Just curious.

GIRL: Not really. I mean, when I used to see Jesus in those Easter movies I thought he was cool. Like how he walked on water and whatnot. There was this one where he turned all this bread into tropical fish and shit. That was pretty dope…Why, do you?

WOMAN: I don't know.

GIRL: What do you believe in, credit cards? Fancy clothes catalogs and shit?

WOMAN: I believe in luck, I guess.

GIRL: Luck.

WOMAN: Yes. Luck.

GIRL: You a gambler?

WOMAN: Sometimes. Not as much as I'd like to be.

GIRL: You should move to Las Vegas.

WOMAN: Maybe I should.

GIRL: Blackjack. Three-card suzie. That's prolly why you don't fly. Luck.

WOMAN: It's true. I have this fear that things would go bad for me on a plane. That I'd lose myself somehow.

GIRL: That's how I feel about fuckin' trains. I kept tellin' Morris we shoulda drove. Nigga just bought a '99 BMW.

WOMAN: Is Morris the father?

GIRL: I think so.

WOMAN: Where were you two planning on going?

GIRL: I don't know. Somewhere west. Like the ocean maybe. Swim with the starfish. Chill with the electric eels and shit. He said he had a partner out there. On some beach with a Italian name.

WOMAN: Venice Beach.

GIRL: Yeah, Venice Beach.

WOMAN: Well, wherever you wind up I wish you luck, Exley.
    She doesn't respond. It's as if I've stung her. Sure, an overly educated, more fortunate white woman in designer clothes can just throw Luck around. It's a mild luxury like potpourri or expensive soap.
    When the conductor re-enters I tell him how Exley may be hemorrhaging from her uterus and he calls the paramedics on his walkie-talkie.
    She is staring out the window as if there is something in the barren fields that will pardon her. As if there is a fairy tale about poor white girls that has yet to be written.
    We lock eyes for a moment. Bravely. Somehow longingly. I never used to believe that strangers shared these kind of moments. Those café scenes in French films. The intimate camera angle. The chamber music. It all adds so much. Even in novels. The description of the fading light. The moon hidden in the prose. In real life these exchanges are simply anecdotes. Little stories that turn into a kind of conversational currency. A four-minute curiosity to be tweaked and shaped. But nothing more. It's never about yearning or frailty or pure, wordless human contact.
    By the time the train stops in Indiana Exley has lost consciousness. There is an enormous volume of blood pooling in her lap. When the doors open there are policemen. There are station managers. There are paramedics as silent as aliens. Far too many men to move the body of a small, lifeless girl.
    I tell one of the paramedics that I think it's a botched abortion. I give him the number where I'm staying and ask him to call me. To let me know how she makes it through.
    That evening I move my things into the café car and eat the tasteless food and continue line editing my young author's clumsy first novel. I sleep restlessly in a clenched seated position.
    Two days later I arrive on the West Coast and my publishing friend picks me up in a Range Rover. Howard Slutes has shaved his moustache and I don't like it. I don't like his hands or his mouth or

those little bumps on his neck, either. But despite my misgivings we feign mutual romantic interest and drink a bottle of wine and perform clinical sexual intercourse in the froth of the Pacific Ocean. Out of loneliness more than anything else. Why I have to travel across the country to make love to a man I barely know I have no idea. Is it ambition? Or ego? Or the need to collect a story? Maybe it's some kind of absurd attempt at preservation of the species? Plain old-fashioned animal fucking. An ape fuck. Perhaps it's the simple need to get away from myself? That's what happens when we cloister off in the city. The years add up like so many forgotten fruit rinds and we're left with the unpleasant mystery of our own sour-smelling skin.

His body is like salty beef. I notice more horrible imperfections. Moles and scars and pockets of flab. He tells me that he has had a vasectomy. His cock is hard and small and when he comes he sounds like a woman. He toots like a clarinet.

We spend the next few days together talking about Graham Greene and the new fall list, which features three of my authors. We continue fucking with a forced inevitability that somehow makes me think of pontoon boats.

A few weeks after I get back to New York I start to feel sick in the mornings. I think I must have gotten a bug from traveling. Something from the other coast. That inexplicable way time zones corrupt the immune system. All that trapped train air.

Three weeks later I miss my period. I am vomiting like a frat boy. I buy an over-the-counter pregnancy test. It turns out positive.

I am two months along now. My breasts have swollen. My appetite has changed. I have told no one. Not even Howard Slutes and his purported vasectomy. When he calls me at work we talk about Graham Greene and the prep school novel. He'll sell it well, he says. The buyers in his region are excited.

I often think of Exley. That paramedic never called me. I don't recall what she did or said so much as her will. How it burned through her skin. That lost white orchid. Did she make it through? Did someone find her at the hospital? A priest? A policeman? A man with a guitar? Is she wandering the snow-swept highways of Indiana?

There are certain hours of the night when I wake to the sound of a train. It roars right through my apartment. At times it feels as if it will lift me out of bed. All that earsplitting thunder and then silence. A quiet that can't be captured in prose or likened to certain kinds of weather. A calm that defies even thought. Just the purest absence of noise.

Perhaps souls have the ability to leap from womb to womb? Like invisible tree frogs.

I am alone, Exley. I am very much alone in a city that at times makes people feel old and used. But I am somehow lucky. Even during the darkest hour I manage to always pull through...

[*Lights fade.*]

END OF PLAY

WALKIN' BACKWARD

a play in one act

Brian Silberman

Walkin' Backward by Brian Silberman. Copyright © 2002 Brian Silberman. All rights reserved.

CAUTION: Professionals and amateurs are hereby warned that *Walkin' Backward* by Brian Silberman is subject to a royalty. It is fully protected under the copyright laws of the United States of America, and of all countries covered by the International Copyright Union (including the Dominion of Canada and the rest of the British Commonwealth), and of all countries covered by the Pan-American Copyright Convention and the Universal Copyright Convention, and of all countries with which the United States has reciprocal copyright relations. All rights, including professional, amateur, motion picture, recitation, lecturing, public reading, radio broadcasting, television, video or sound taping, all other forms of mechanical or electronic reproduction, such as information storage and retrieval systems and photo-copyright, and the rights of translation into foreign languages are strictly reserved. Particular emphasis is laid upon the question of readings, permission for which must be secured from the author's agent in writing.

Inquiries concerning all performing rights to the play should be addressed to the author's agent, Ronald Gwiazda, ROSENSTONE/WENDER, 38 East 29th Street, New York, New York 10016.

Brian Silberman

BRIAN SILBERMAN'S *Walkin' Backward* is the first of a larger, five-play cycle of one-act plays about orphans and abandonment in a small Virginia town, collectively entitled *The Buckland Canticle*. His other plays include *Manifest*, recipient of the 1998 Clauder Prize, *Sugar Down Billie Hoak*, *Feral Music*, *Half Court*, *Ambivalent North*, *Salvage Baas*, *Dustbreeding*, *Retrenchment*, and *The Gospel According to Toots Pope*. Currently, Mr. Silberman teaches dramatic writing at Old Dominion University.

And so as the old die and the young
depart, where shall a man go who keeps
the memories of the dead, except home
again, as one would go back after a burial,
faithful to the fields, lest the dead die
a second and more final death.

—Wendell Berry
At a Country Funeral

Even the refugee must do more than flee.
He must arrive.

—Tim O'Brien
Going after Cacciato

CHARACTERS:

MONKEY HILL, age 16
COONEY WEBSTER, age 13
ROSS BURCHETT, age 14

SETTING:

Railroad tracks in Buckland, Virginia, a small back-country town.
Mid-July, 1965. Noon. A set of decrepit railroad tracks stretch
across a small section of Virginia flatland. Rocks have been built up
slightly into a running mound, to raise the track from a circle of
earth. The tracks themselves are in disrepair, the ties rotted and
split, the rails, having lost some of their spikes, curled and twisted
off-center. In several places the rails bow out and away from the line
of ties. The heat of the mid-July sun bears down oppressively; the
whistling drone of cicadas is heard in the breezeless air.

[*At rise,* COONEY WEBSTER, MONKEY HILL, *and* ROSS
BURCHETT *move along the railroad tracks,* ROSS *and* COONEY *up
front, each walking "tight rope" on a rail, their arms outstretched for balance,*
MONKEY *behind, moving them along. They are dressed in their dark Sunday
suits, collars open, shirttails out.*]

ROSS: [*Singing "The Wreck of the Old 97."*] "They gave him his orders at Monroe, Virginia, saying 'Engineer you're way behind time. This ain't the 38, it's Ol' 97, 'n ya got ta put her in Spencer on time.' So he looks roun' ta his coalman 'n then at his watch 'n says 'Boys shovel in some more coal. It's a mighty rough line from Lynchburgh ta Danville, but jus' watch this ol' 97 roll.' She's speedin' down grade on the way inta Danville when the whistle breaks inta a scream. Train flew off the track 'n was found in a wreck, the men a-scalded ta death by the steam."

[*He stops, glancing up at the sun, then taking off his jacket. He pulls at his necktie, loosening it, and glances up at* COONEY, *who has continued moving along the rail.*]

Sure was nice.

COONEY: [*Concentrating on his balance.*] Yup.

ROSS: Nice fer a funeral.

MONKEY: Too hot out.

COONEY: Yup.

MONKEY: Yer momma sure picked a hot day ta git buried on, Cooney.

COONEY: [*Still concentrating fiercely.*] Reckon she did.

MONKEY: Hotter 'n hell.

ROSS: She weren't feelin' it.
She looked real good, don't ya think, Cooney?

COONEY: Yup.

ROSS: Looked real nice there in that box.

MONKEY: Not ta me.

ROSS: Looked real good.

MONKEY: She's dead. What the hell difference do it make what she looked like in the damn box?

ROSS: I'm sayin' it fer Cooney. 'Cause it's his momma.

MONKEY: Ain't nobody gonna be lookin' at her no more.

COONEY: I will.

MONKEY: Ya gonna go 'n dig her up, Cooney?

COONEY: In my head. I mean, lookin' at her in my head.

MONKEY: I hope so, 'cause that's the only place she gonna be from now on.

ROSS: Hey, Monk. How much more ya figure we got?

MONKEY: Ten, 'leven miles.

COONEY: [*Stopping momentarily.*] 'Leven miles?

MONKEY: It ain't too far.

ROSS: It sure is awful hot ta be goin' 'leven miles.

MONKEY: Burchett, you a man or ain't ya?

ROSS: I'm jus' sayin' it's awful hot.

MONKEY: 'Cause you're makin' me think things with all that.

COONEY: [*Resuming his tight rope walk.*] Where we goin', anyways?

MONKEY: Never ya mind.

ROSS: Big secret.

COONEY: Why we goin' then?

MONKEY: Teach ya somethin'.

COONEY: What?

MONKEY: Never ya mind right now. You'll know when we git there.

ROSS: Ya ain't gonna tell us?

MONKEY: Soon enough.

COONEY: [*Stepping off the rail.*] Well, I ain't goin' no 'leven miles 'less I know where I'm goin'.

MONKEY: Why not?

COONEY: 'Cause I jus' ain't.

ROSS: It's awful hot out, Monk.

MONKEY: Goddamn.

COONEY: Cain't jus' go off 'leven miles down the tracks fer no reason.

MONKEY: There's a reason.

ROSS: Cain't jus' go off somewheres the day a' his momma's funeral.

MONKEY: Why not? She ain't there ta tell 'im he cain't.

COONEY: I gotta sit. My asthmer's comin' on.

MONKEY: Jesus H.

COONEY: I can feel it.

MONKEY: You 'n yer goddamn asthmer.

> [COONEY *sits, taking an inhaler from his pocket. He takes a deep pull on the mouthpiece.* ROSS *goes to help him.*]

ROSS: It's the heat. Makes it come out. It'll be all right.

[*He starts massaging* COONEY's *chest.*]

I gotta rub his chest fer him like this 'n it gits better.

MONKEY: Goddamn.

ROSS: Maybe we oughta take a break.

MONKEY: Aaw, goddamn.

ROSS: Take a break 'n eat somethin'.

MONKEY: We jus' started.

[ROSS *pulls a large chunk of cake wrapped in a napkin from his pocket.*]

ROSS: I got some a' that cake from the church.

COONEY: [*Turning to* ROSS.] Gimme some.

ROSS: Got some apples too.

COONEY: What kinda cake is it?

ROSS: Ya want an apple, Monk?

COONEY: [*Taking the cake from* ROSS.] S' it chocolate?

[ROSS *pulls two apples from another pocket, tossing one to* MONKEY *and then biting into the other himself.* COONEY *hurriedly unwraps the cake.*]

MONKEY: Five minutes. That's it. We're restin' fer five minutes.

COONEY: [*Breaking off a large piece and eating it.*] Angel food.

MONKEY: Look'it ya. Stuffin' yer face. What about yer damn asthmer?

COONEY: It's over.

ROSS: When he rests it goes away. 'N when I rub his chest.

MONKEY: We ain't stoppin' every ten minutes 'cause a' yer damn asthmer.

COONEY: Maybe I ain't gonna go then.

MONKEY: Y'are too goin'.

COONEY: No, I ain't.

ROSS: 'Less ya tell us where.

COONEY: Yeah, I ain't goin' 'less ya says where.

MONKEY: Fine. Manassas Junction.

COONEY: What?

MONKEY: Manassas Junction.

ROSS: How come?

MONKEY: 'Cause I say.

COONEY: We're goin' where?

MONKEY: Ta see where Stoney Jackson 'n the Rebels derailed a train off the old O&A.

COONEY: The what?

ROSS: The old Orange 'n Alexandria line. It's fer trains.

MONKEY: Alexandria ta Gordonsville.

[ROSS *prostrates himself on the tracks, laying his head on a rail.*]

ROSS: [*Singing.*] "I'm gonna lay my head on the railroad line. Let the O 'n A ease my troubled mind."

COONEY: Why y'all want ta be goin' ta that ol' junction anyways?

[MONKEY *shakes his head and moves forward along the rail.*]

MONKEY: Nah. I done tol' enough.

ROSS: How come ya wanna go there so bad?

MONKEY: Jus' 'cause.

COONEY: That ain't no reason.

MONKEY: I done told ya more 'n ya need ta know already.

COONEY: [*Sitting down on the rail in defiance.*] Well, I'm gonna sit down right here 'n not go no further 'til ya tell how come.

[MONKEY *throws away his apple core and makes as if to move on.*]

MONKEY: Fine. Y'all be sittin' there when Burchett 'n me git back.

COONEY: Will not.

MONKEY: So what if ya ain't?

ROSS: Maybe I ain't goin' neither.

MONKEY: Aaw, goddamn it all ta hell.

ROSS: I ain't gonna go if Cooney don't. What if he got 'nother spell a' his asthmer? I gotta rub his chest.

MONKEY: He can rub his own damn chest.

ROSS: I got to.

COONEY: Tell it.

ROSS: Ya ain't gonna win.

[MONKEY *throws up his arms.*]

MONKEY: Jesus H. Christ. Y'all 're a big ol' pain in my ass, ya know that?

COONEY: Tell it.

MONKEY: Gotta know everythin' straight off.

COONEY: Tell it.

MONKEY: It's the war. The Civil War. 'N that Union gen'ral…Gen'ral Haupt was a comin' down the O&A with a load a supplies fer Gen'ral McDowell ta git Stonewall Jackson with at Bull Run. 'N ol' Stonewall…he had ta git hisself, 'cause he didn't have no more ammo 'n was a-fearin' gittin' his men whipped. So, Stoney 'n the Confeds started beatin' it the hell outta Manassas…'n they tore up the tracks 'n set fire ta the bridge outside a' the junction 'fore they left, figurin' they'd slow up them Yanks fer a' coupla days 'n save their skins. 'Cept they was rushin' so much, they done blowed the bridge 'fore they got all a' their own trains over…'n two of 'em…two a' them Confed trains hit the twisted up track 'n derailed by the bridge. Kill't a bunch a' their own Confeds, right then.

COONEY: Kill't 'em?

MONKEY: Most.

COONEY: What happened ta the rest?

MONKEY: Ol' Stonewall 'n all them other Confed trains jus' kept right on a-going 'cause a' Gen'ral McDowell 'n them Union troops…plus, they couldn't a' gotten back 'cross that bridge nohow. So, they jus' left 'em there. Marooned 'em.

ROSS: Marooned 'em, all right.

COONEY: [*Echoing softly.*] Marooned.

MONKEY: Yup. Left 'em all ta die. Their own kin almost…yer fightin' buddies is yer own kin almost…'n they jus' up 'n left 'em. Up 'n left 'em ta die.

[COONEY *rises.*]

COONEY: And it's really a wreck? Where we're a-goin'?

MONKEY: What'd I jus' tell ya? Yeah, it's a wreck.

COONEY: S' there gonna be bones 'n dead bodies all around?

ROSS: Don't be dumb, Cooney. It's from a long time ago…there ain't gonna be no dead people.

COONEY: I bet there's ghosts though. If their ain't no dead people, there's gonna be ghosts of 'em.

ROSS: Nah.

COONEY: Buncha friggin' ghosts.

ROSS: Don't be dumb.

COONEY: Bet there is. I'll bet there is too ghosts out there. Ain't that right, Monkey? Ain't there gonna be ghosts?

MONKEY: Could be.

COONEY: [*To* ROSS.] See?

MONKEY: I'd be a ghost if'n I was on one a' them Confed trains. I'd be a-hauntin' all up 'n down these tracks fer what they done.

COONEY: I wouldn't. I'd be up in heaven listenin' ta ol' Gabe a-blowin' on his horn and a-tappin' my feet and a-drinkin' nectars 'n gittin' fanned by girly angels.

MONKEY: I'd be spookin' every last one a' them bastard Confeds that left me behind.

COONEY: Not me. I'd be drinkin' nectars from big ol' gold pots them girly angels were a-givin' me.

MONKEY: Spookin'.

ROSS: We're goin' 'leven miles ta see them Confed ghosts? That why we're goin'?

MONKEY: We're goin' a-'cause both a' ya don't know nothin'.

[COONEY *leaps up on a rail and begins moving on the "tight rope" toward Manassas.*]

COONEY: I'm goin' ta see me a ghost.

ROSS: Fine.

COONEY: I'll balance race somebody.

MONKEY: [*Stepping up on a rail.*] I'll balance race ya backwards.

COONEY: [*Stopping.*] Huh?

MONKEY: Bet ya I win too. Me walkin' backwards 'n ya goin' frontways.

[*He gets even with* COONEY *on the rail.*]

Go.

[*They begin racing.*]

ROSS: My momma says I cain't walk backwards.

MONKEY: [*Stopping.*] Sure ya can.

ROSS: She won't let me. Says that's how the dead walk 'n she won't let me.

MONKEY: It's what?

ROSS: It's how the dead walk.

COONEY: Yeah?

MONKEY: Dead folks don't walk backwards. That's dumb.

ROSS: My momma says.

MONKEY: Then yer momma's dumb. Dead folks don't walk backwards, they walk frontways jus' like we do. Only difference is they walk behind us live folks. Followin' us.

[COONEY *turns to look behind him.*]

COONEY: I don't see nothin'.

MONKEY: I do. See, dead folks they ain't got no lungs in 'em so they cain't yell fer ya ta turn 'round or nothin'. But they want ya to. That's why I walk backwards. 'Cause if'n ya walk backwards yer seein' 'em 'n they can look at yer face.

ROSS: That ain't what my momma says.

COONEY: [*To* MONKEY.] Ya think I can see me a ghost when we get ta Manassas?

MONKEY: Ya'll don't know squat 'bout ghosts…'bout what it means ta be a ghost.

COONEY: Do so.

ROSS: Cooney's ma's a ghost.

COONEY: She's an angel ghost.

MONKEY: Angel ghost? There ain't no such thing. See what I mean? Ya don't know squat. Cooney's ma's a damn angel ghost? Ya don't know nothin'. I'm teachin' ya. You're gonna see them Confeds that got marooned. S' gonna make ya see.

ROSS: See what?

MONKEY: What dead is.

COONEY: I'm gonna see me one a' them Confed ghosts.

ROSS: Y'are not.

MONKEY: There's ghosts up 'n down this track. 'N ya'll don't even know.

COONEY: [*Echoing.*] All up 'n down.

MONKEY: Railroad's a good place ta be a ghost too. 'Cause it's a mean ol' place. Jus' look at all the criminals 'n no-goods live out on the rails.

COONEY: Jesse James.

ROSS: Butch 'n Sundance.

MONKEY: Railroad Bill Scruggs.

[ROSS *moves along the tracks, suddenly inspired, leaping from tie to tie, singing loudly, timing the song's phrases with his leaps.*]

ROSS: "Railroad Bill..." [*Leap.*] "ought ta be killed..." [*Leap.*] "never worked a day..." [*Leap.*] "and he never will. Railroad Bill done took my wife, threatened to me that he'd take my life. Buy me a gun jus' as long as my arm, kill everybody ever done me wrong. Goin' up on the mountain, take my stand, thirty-eight special in my right 'n left hand. If the river was whiskey 'n I was a divin' duck, I'd sink ta the bottom—"

MONKEY: Ya walk like a divin' duck, ya know that Burchett? Duck-footed.

ROSS: Do not.

MONKEY: Whole Burchett family walks duck-footed. Must be somethin' in the blood.

ROSS: [*Looking down at his feet as he walks.*] I do not walk duck-footed.

MONKEY: All yer kin walk that way.

COONEY: Like a buncha ducks.

ROSS: Shut up, Cooney.

COONEY: Buncha friggin' ducks. Quack! Quack!

MONKEY: Least he ain't got droopy eyes like you Websters. Looks like you're all retarded.

COONEY: Does not.

MONKEY: Sure as hell does.

ROSS: And yer kin's all perfect, huh Monk?

MONKEY: Damned straight it is.

COONEY: They're all stiffs.

MONKEY: So?

COONEY: Buncha friggin' stiffs.

MONKEY: That's why they're perfect. See? They ain't even there. They're dead.

COONEY: Jus' like my momma is. Perfect like a angel.

MONKEY: What'd I tell you 'bout that?

[MONKEY *moves off and sits. There is a pause. He pulls out a book of matches and strikes one, staring intently at the flame.*]

ROSS: Ya miss 'em, Monkey? Yer folks?

MONKEY: Nah.

ROSS: Not even yer momma?

MONKEY: I didn't even know my momma.

[ROSS *sits beside* MONKEY.]

ROSS: I know, but do ya miss not havin' her?

COONEY: Buncha friggin' momma.

MONKEY: Will ya quit that?

COONEY: Ya cain't make me.

MONKEY: [*Stepping toward* COONEY.] Yeah?

[COONEY *backs away quietly.*]

ROSS: I would, I think. If'n my momma'd died when I was born. I'd miss her. My daddy too.

MONKEY: [*Sitting.*] Hell, I probably wouldn't a' cared much fer neither of 'em. They'd always be yellin' at me or a-callin' after me…or fightin' each other all the time or somethin'…

ROSS: Maybe.

MONKEY: Fightin' like them foster parents I got, Ol' Man 'n Ol' Lady Ransom, do.

COONEY: Hell, they fight like all git out.

MONKEY: That's why I got free a' them.

ROSS: Yeah?

MONKEY: Ol' Man Ransom, he's always gittin' mad at his ol' lady.

COONEY: [*Sitting beside the other two.*] Always.

MONKEY: Ya don't see it, Burchett, livin' like ya do. The ol' man is always gittin' down his shotgun 'n tryin' ta shoot her. Shoot his own ol' lady. Don't even pay fer me ta care fer 'em, 'cause pretty soon he ain't gonna miss. 'N then they both might as well be dead. That's why I ran away.

ROSS: When?

MONKEY: Now. Right now.

ROSS: Damn.

MONKEY: I see enough a' them foster homes ta know my own kin ain't a' been no different. Hell, it's good they died on me. Did me a favor a' not havin' nothin' like that goin' on.

COONEY: The ol' man beat the hell outa Mrs. Ransom last week. I saw it.

ROSS: How come?

COONEY: Said he had ta, on account a' 'cause she'd ducked outta his sights when he put the gun on her 'n made him blow a big hole in their new Chevrolet.

ROSS: That right, Monk?

[MONKEY *removes his necktie and ties it around his head.*]

MONKEY: I'd rather be on my own like I am. 'S not worth havin' folks fer somethin' like that.

ROSS: They mighta been good though. Yer own momma mighta been good.

MONKEY: Yeah, but she mighta not.

COONEY: You ain't never gonna know, Monk, 'cause ya kill't her.

MONKEY: [*Angered.*] She died 'cause a' childbirth. Childbirth, all right? I didn't do nothin'.

COONEY: Well, you was the child got birthed.

MONKEY: Shut up, Cooney. Ya know what I mean. Weren't nothin' I coulda done about it.

COONEY: I guess so.

MONKEY: I know so. So shut up.

[*There is a slight pause.*]

ROSS: Where ya running away ta, Monk?

MONKEY: Jus' away is all.

COONEY: [*Echoing.*] Away.

ROSS: But where?

MONKEY: Somewhere else, I reckon.

[*There is a pause.*]

ROSS: You runnin' off 'n Cooney's ma's funeral on the same day. That's somethin'.

MONKEY: I reckon.

ROSS: Seeing dead folks musta put it in yer head, huh Monk?

MONKEY: Dead folks do that.

COONEY: [*Softly.*] Buncha friggin' dead folks.

ROSS: That was the first dead person I ever seen fer real.

MONKEY: I seen lots.

ROSS: Did ya see yer own daddy when he was dead?

MONKEY: I was there, but I ain't seen him. Hell, I was what, one years old? I wouldn't a' even know'd he was dead if'n I had a' seen him.

ROSS: I reckon not.

MONKEY: I was one years old. What am I supposed ta know 'bout dead folks then?

ROSS: Nothin' I guess.

MONKEY: Learned me quick though, I reckon.

ROSS: Quicker 'n ya shoulda.

MONKEY: I seen dead people 'fore today though.

COONEY: Have not.

MONKEY: Have so. 'Member them two brothers that died…drowned?

ROSS: Clem 'n Pete Charles.

MONKEY: Yup. I was in the sixth grade 'n Mizz Johnson walked us all down there ta the river ta watch the fire 'n rescue draggin' at the water.

ROSS: Mean ol' Mizzes Jacob wouldn't let the fourth grade go.

MONKEY: There'd a' been four of 'em ya know. Jeep Early, Pepper Watson, and then Clem 'n Pete. 'N Jeep 'n Pepper'd done got out fine, but them brothers were still in the river somewheres.

ROSS: A-lyin' on the bottom.

MONKEY: That's right.

COONEY: [*Echoing.*] On the bottom.

MONKEY: They'd all done hooked school, see.

ROSS: That's right. Hooked.

MONKEY: Figured they'd go down ta the river on accounta it bein' such a hot day…splash 'round some 'n cool off their feet. But they musta done swum out some…swum out inta that water where the current was strong…too strong…'n it done took hold 'n sunk 'em.

COONEY: Buncha friggin' current.

MONKEY: I saw 'em fish ol' Clem 'n then ol' Pete up outta the river 'n onta the bank.

ROSS: Goddamn.

MONKEY: Saw 'em fish 'em out dead.

COONEY: [*Echoing.*] Goddamn.

MONKEY: Mizz Johnson, she went over ta look if it was sure…if it was right sure there weren't nothin' ta be done could get life back inta them two boys. But they musta been dead right fine enough, 'cause she just turned 'n walked us all back up ta school.

[*There is a slight pause.*]

COONEY: What'd they look like, them two boys?

MONKEY: Like they was dead.

COONEY: They look all swelled up 'n puffy 'n stuff?

MONKEY: Nah, jus' dead, that's all. Looked the same at the funeral. Dead. Even all dressed up they still looked dead.

[*He stops for a moment, remembering.*]

Shoulda seen how their momma carried on though, a-cryin' and a-wailin' fer all git out. That was nice. I saw it…'n if'n I was Clem or Pete I woulda loved my momma fer that. It was sure fine how she missed them boys.

COONEY: Buncha friggin' missin'.

MONKEY: That's right.

[*There is a slight pause.*]

COONEY: My momma today looked like she was sleepin'. Ain't that right, Monkey? Jus' like she was a-sleepin'.

MONKEY: Yer momma looked dead as them two boys ta me.

COONEY: Oh.

[*There is a pause.* COONEY *moves off slightly.*]

ROSS: My momma 'n daddy had a baby that died.

MONKEY: Ya see it?

ROSS: Nah…I didn't. It was 'fore I was born. They tol' me 'bout it though. A baby girl.

MONKEY: What happened to her?

ROSS: Don't know. Never got ta breathin', my daddy said.

COONEY: Never breathin'?

ROSS: I think about it sometimes…that baby girl…'n seein' Cooney's momma today made me think on it again…'bout what it'd be like ta have me a sister. 'Cause I got this pit'chure of my momma 'n daddy in my head…after it happened.

COONEY: What kinda pit'chure?

ROSS: Two a' them in that hospital room…fussin' over their new baby girl…'n she's pink 'n breathin' just fine.

MONKEY: [*To* COONEY.] See? Jus' like I told ya. Dead.

ROSS: I don't like thinkin' on it too much. 'Cause I'm scared a how much want they got inside, even now…jus' ta say, "daughter…daughter."

[ROSS *kicks at the ground with his foot. There is a pause.*]

COONEY: My daddy, every time he went off workin' somewheres far away, brung things back fer me. 'Til one time, the bag from the Woolworth's in Spencer had a hatchet inside… a big ol' hatchet 'n one a' them stones fer honin' the blade. 'N my daddy… he done took me out ta the yard, sayin' fer me ta start sharpenin' it up some. 'N I tried… I did… dragged it on that stone somethin' fierce... done it 'til I cried... but I couldn't get that hatchet sharp. 'N no matter what he did... how much my daddy tried 'n yelled 'n cussed 'n hit... I jus' couldn't get that edge ta come like he wanted. No matter what. 'Til he jus' grabbed that ol' hatchet 'n took it away.

[*He pauses slightly.*]

'N it didn't take longer fer me ta figure... next time my daddy went off workin' somewheres far away, he weren't gonna be comin' back with nothin' fer me.

MONKEY: Yer daddy's a no good thing anyway. He's a drunk 'n a criminal. White trash. I wouldn't want nothin' from him nohow.

COONEY: He weren't always like that, ya know.

MONKEY: Fer a long time he was. Ever since he knocked off Jake Bushey behind McGavick's IGA he was. Ever since he's doin' time in prison he was.

COONEY: Yeah, I guess.

MONKEY: Damn right. And he's gonna stay that way too. Gonna die in prison a drunk 'n a criminal.

COONEY: Unh-unh.

MONKEY: Well, he ain't never gonna git out, lessin' he jailbreaks.

ROSS: Y'all hear 'bout Deetum Rooney? He went on jailbreak.

MONKEY: Who ain't a heard 'bout him?

ROSS: Ever since ol' Deetum done broke outta prison, my momma's took ta sleepin' with all the windows locked up tight.

MONKEY: Deetum Rooney's a crazyman. Jus' look at him.

COONEY: Aw, Monkey Hill, ya ain't never seen no sign a' Deetum Rooney.

MONKEY: Have so.

ROSS: I never seen him, 'cept in my head. But he was damn sure crazy-lookin' all right when I imagined him.

MONKEY: Got no insides 'cause he ate 'em all.

COONEY: He sure ain't not ate his own insides.

MONKEY: Says you.

COONEY: Buncha friggin' lies.

ROSS: Bud Phelps at school was tellin' me 'bout Deetum helpin' his daddy work a still up on Coots Ridge.

MONKEY: [*Nodding.*] Moonshiners.

ROSS: Then…one day Bud ain't in school. 'N everybody said Deetum had done kill't 'n ate him 'n his whole family fer supper.

COONEY: Git out.

ROSS: Chopped 'em up with a shovel 'n ate all the pieces. But Bud was back ta school the next day 'n straightened us out. Said Deetum 'n his daddy done had words 'bout the moonshinin' money.

[MONKEY *sneaks up behind* COONEY.]

'N Deetum grabbed up this big ol' shovel over his head 'n brung it down hard.

[MONKEY *jumps* COONEY *from behind, his arm swinging down on* COONEY'*s head like an axe.*]

MONKEY: Shovel comin' down right on the middle of Ol' Man Phelps' skull!

ROSS: Whunk!

MONKEY: Goddamn did!

COONEY: [*In disbelief.*] Go on!

MONKEY: [*Nodding and releasing* COONEY.] S' true.

ROSS: And Bud said weren't nobody seen Deetum Rooney since. But that the Sheriff was lookin' real hard. Had the whole police out.

[*There is a slight pause.*]

COONEY: Well, they git him or what? They catch that crazy Deetum Rooney?

MONKEY: Not right then.

ROSS: No sir.

MONKEY: [*Leaping on* ROSS's *back.*] 'Cause ol' Deetum, he took off fer the hills… 'n ain't nobody gonna catch him when he takes ta the hills.

[ROSS *gallops around the tracks with* MONKEY *on his back.*]

COONEY: Buncha friggin' hills!

MONKEY: Ain't nobody gonna catch him.

ROSS: Not until the stench leads 'em to him.

MONKEY: That's right.

COONEY: Huh?

[MONKEY *climbs off* ROSS's *back, and crouches beside the tracks.*]

MONKEY: Ol' Deetum gits it into his head ta git his hands on a shipment a' seafood 'n unload it ta restaurants 'n the like. Then he can git some cash 'n make his getaway in style, see. Which is all well 'n good, 'cepting where's he goin' ta git a shipment a' seafood?

COONEY: [*Crouching too.*] Where?

ROSS: Hijacks this eighteen-wheeler out on the expressway.

MONKEY: Flags some poor trucker down with a rifle, then throws him outa his truck.

ROSS: Refrigerated truck full a' butterfly shrimp. Regent Seafood Comp'ny.

MONKEY: Said it right on the truck. That's how he knew. "Regent Seafood Comp'ny."

ROSS: Ol' Deetum climbs on in 'n takes it down the highway, stoppin' here 'n there, trying ta unload the stuff at restaurants. Takes it all the way ta Richmond. But he's got jus' tons a' them butterfly shrimps 'n he jus' couldn't sell 'em all.

MONKEY: [*Laying on the tracks.*] And he's hidin' out all this time too. Layin' low.

[COONEY *"lays low" on the tracks alongside* MONKEY.]

ROSS: After about a week it starts a-goin' bad on him.

MONKEY: Starts stinkin' ta high heaven.

ROSS: Yup.

MONKEY: Well, there's jus' so much goddamn butterfly shrimp ya can take.

COONEY: Buncha friggin' shrimp.

MONKEY: Well, ol' Deetum don't know what the Christ he's gonna do with it all. And he's still got this stolen truck on his hands.

ROSS: 'Course he figured on unloadin' it all in one swoop.

MONKEY: Stupid bastard.

ROSS: So, he drives back up here, takes it up into the mountains, up ta High Knob, 'n spends all night with this stolen backhoe diggin' a great big trench. Then in the mornin', he drives the whole truck right into it.

COONEY: The whole friggin' truck?

ROSS: That's right.

MONKEY: Then fills it back in.

ROSS: Goddamn does.

COONEY: [*Echoing.*] Goddamn.

MONKEY: Woulda worked out all right too, 'cept he didn't bury it all that deep.

ROSS: Didn't bury it deep enough ta keep the smell from gittin' through.

MONKEY: 'N pretty soon there's these flocks of gulls circlin' all around High Knob.

ROSS: Friggin' seagulls flyin' all around High Knob.

COONEY: Buncha friggin' seagulls.

MONKEY: "Now what in the name a Christ is seagulls doin' at High Knob, more'n a hundred miles from the ocean?" people are a-sayin'. The sheriff, he goes out ta take a look 'n after he's about a hundred yards away, he knows right where them stolen shrimps are a-hidin'.

ROSS: Sure does.

MONKEY: Found good ol' Deetum close by too, all tanked up on moonshine, depressed 'cause his plan went ta hell.

ROSS: That'll teach ya about stealin' anythin'.

MONKEY: Least about stealin' shrimps.

[*There is a slight pause.*]

ROSS: Ol' Deetum is sure right crazy though.

MONKEY: Crazy enough ta make hisself a jailbreak.

ROSS: Kill't two guards with jus' his bare hands.

MONKEY: Crazy like a fox.

[*There is a pause.*]

You know…I wouldn't be surprised if'n ol' Deetum's out on the rails right now.

COONEY: Ya think so?

MONKEY: I'll bet ol' Deetum's close.

COONEY: He ain't not.

MONKEY: Could be.

[*He climbs up on a rail.*]

We best keep moving so's he don't git us sittin' around.

ROSS: Maybe ol' Deetum's goin' ta Manassus too.

COONEY: What'd he be there fer?

MONKEY: Same as us.

COONEY: I ain't goin' if'n he's there too.

ROSS: He ain't gonna be there, Cooney.

[MONKEY *squats down on his haunches, putting his ear to the train rail.*]

COONEY: Whatcha listenin' fer?

MONKEY: Shh.

COONEY: S' it Deetum?

MONKEY: Nope.

COONEY: What is it?

MONKEY: It's ol' Gen'ral Haupt comin' down the rails.

ROSS: Is he comin'?

MONKEY: I reckon so.

[COONEY *puts his ear to the rail.*]

COONEY: I don't hear nothin'.

MONKEY: He's a-comin' all right.

[*He jumps up quickly, now one of the Confederate soldiers of his story.*]

Quick, Burchett, we gotta blow the rails.

ROSS: [*Playing along.*] Yup. We'd sure better.

MONKEY: We need us some dynamite.

COONEY: I don't hear nothin'.

[MONKEY *begins picking up rocks and sticks from the ground and laying them along the rails. ROSS joins him.*]

MONKEY: He's a-comin' up quick.

ROSS: Sure is.

COONEY: [*Standing.*] Ain't nothin' comin' nowheres.

MONKEY: [*To ROSS.*] We better haul ass. He'll be right on us.

[*He lays out the remainder of his rocks.*]

This'll do it. Ya ready ta blow yers?

ROSS: Yep.

MONKEY: Better git back.

COONEY: Buncha friggin' nothin'.

[MONKEY *and* ROSS *move off quickly, throwing themselves down on the ground and covering their heads.*]

MONKEY: Five…four…

[ROSS *joins the countdown.*]

ROSS: Three…

COONEY: Ain't nothin' comin'.

MONKEY: Two…

ROSS: One.

MONKEY: KAAABOOOOOOMM!!!

ROSS: BAAAMM!!

[ROSS *and* MONKEY *leap wildly up and down making loud, explosive noises.*]

MONKEY: POW! Look at that bridge go up!

ROSS: BLAM! There goes the tracks!

MONKEY: All twisted 'n blow'd up! WHOOOM!

ROSS: Wrecked ta hell!

MONKEY: Blow'd ta kingdom come!

ROSS: Sure are.

COONEY: You guys are dumb.

MONKEY: Them Yanks is gonna have some kinda time gittin' 'cross now.

COONEY: Ain't nothin' comin' 'n them tracks're the same as they jus' was.

MONKEY: Oh yeah?

COONEY: Yeah.

MONKEY: Says who?

COONEY: Says me.

MONKEY: Well, we'll jus' see about that.

[MONKEY *rushes* COONEY, *grabbing him from behind and pinning his arms. He pulls* COONEY's *jacket up and over his head, blinding him.* COONEY *struggles but cannot get free.*]

COONEY: Quit it! Git off'a me!

MONKEY: Burchett, git his feet. Git his feet.

[ROSS *takes* COONEY'S *feet. He now lies stretched in the air between the two.*]

COONEY: Leggo a' me! Git off!

MONKEY: Ya sure them tracks're still there?

ROSS: [*Laughing.*] I think ya best say they's busted up, Cooney.

COONEY: Yer chokin' me! Git off, I said!

MONKEY: Ya real sure? Yer one a' them Confeds, Cooney. 'N Gen'ral Haupt is a-comin' up quick. Watch out!

[*He imitates a train whistle.*]

"Whooo! Whooo!" Ya hear that?

COONEY: Git off'a me!

MONKEY: Train whistle. There he is. Damn, we gotta move. Shee-it, he's right around the bend.

[*He begins swinging* COONEY *by the arms, simulating the motion of a train,* ROSS *joining in with the feet.*]

We better steam up our engines 'n beat it the hell outta here.

COONEY: Quit that!

MONKEY: She needs more coal. Burchett, shovel more coal.

[*He swings* COONEY *with more force, building as the train increases speed.*]

"Whooo! Whooo!" He's real close now.

COONEY: Leggo a' my legs!

MONKEY: You're the last train, Cooney. You're the last one.

[*He begins shaking* COONEY *violently.*]

You're steamin' fast as ya can. Jus' a little more 'n yer all right. BOOOM! There's the bridge.

COONEY: [*Growing more frantic.*] Stop it! I'm gonna have my asthmer.

MONKEY: They done blow'd the bridge on ya. "Wait! Wait!" you're a-yellin', "I ain't got 'crossed! Don't blow nothin' yet!" BOOOM! There go the tracks.

[*With each explosion he shakes* COONEY *wildly up and down.* COONEY *begins to wheeze, his asthma coming on.*]

Gen'ral Haupt's right on yer tail. Whatcha gonna do? BOOOM! You're speedin' fast. BOOOM! They blow everythin' on ya.

COONEY: Stoooppppp!

MONKEY: But ya can't stop, Cooney. Ya can't. You're goin' too fast. BOOOM! And them tracks jus' blow'd up in yer face, all twisted 'n bust up.

[*He swings* COONEY *with abandon.* COONEY *begins to cry and wheeze out of desperation.*]

Ya hit 'em goin' full out!

COONEY: Aaaaaahhhh!

MONKEY: All them other trains, all yer buddies are lookin' back at ya from 'cross the bridge. Ya hit them busted tracks 'n ya jus' explode. WHAAAM! You're crashin'. And ya hear all this screamin'.

[COONEY'S *asthma grows worse.* ROSS *becomes concerned.*]

Everybody's all busted up. Gittin' crushed 'n ripped open. And you're yellin', "Wait! Wait!" But ya cain't see nothin' no more 'cause there's too much smoke. And you're rollin' over 'n over, bashin' in everythin'.

ROSS: [*Quietly.*] Monk?

MONKEY: Yer legs git twisted 'n broken off. Yer head splits open 'n all yer brains come flowin' out of it.

COONEY: Momma!

ROSS: Hey, Monk. Stop.

COONEY: Momma!

MONKEY: And you're screamin' fer yer buddies ta come back fer ya, but they ain't comin'.

ROSS: Stop it, Monk.

MONKEY: Nobody's comin', 'cept Gen'ral Haupt 'n them Yankee troops!

ROSS: [*Louder.*] STOP!

[MONKEY *looks at* ROSS, *then releases* COONEY's *hands.* COONEY *falls to the ground, wheezing and crying, his face still covered by his suit jacket.*]

MONKEY: [*Softer.*] And then ya can't hear nothin' no more. 'Cause you're dead. Them bastards left ya on yer own jus' ta die. Marooned ya jus' like it was nothin'. The low-downest snake of a thing. Like yer momma 'n daddy did to ya. Like mine did ta me. You're dependin' on 'em 'n they made ya an orphan jus' like it was nothin'. Took away yer life jus' like it was nothin'. And yer dead. Jus' like them Confeds on the train. You're jus' dead. And ya don't hear nothin'. Ya don't hear nothin'.

[*There is a long pause.* MONKEY *steps away, moving off slowly down the track.* ROSS *bends over* COONEY, *who is curled up in a fetal position. He touches* COONEY's *shoulder*]

ROSS: Y'all right, Cooney?

COONEY: Lemme alone.

ROSS: Lemme rub yer chest fer ya.

[ROSS *leans in to rub his chest, but* COONEY *pushes his hand away.*]

COONEY: Get off.

[COONEY *gets out his inhaler and takes a pull.*]

ROSS: Didn't mean nothin'. Forget it, all right?

MONKEY: He better not forget it.

ROSS: Sorry.

MONKEY: I ain't.

ROSS: We're sorry.

COONEY: Lemme alone.

MONKEY: Aaw, jus' let him cry.

COONEY: Shut up.

[*He sits up, wiping his face with the back of his hand.*]

I wasn't cryin'.

MONKEY: [*Snorting.*] Yeah.

COONEY: I couldn't breathe is all. My asthmer came on. Ya was chokin' me 'n I couldn't breathe.

ROSS: Ya sure?

COONEY: Monkey was chokin' me 'n I couldn't breathe 'cause a' my asthmer.

MONKEY: [*Disgusted.*] Fine.

COONEY: That's what it was. Ya was chokin' me.

MONKEY: [*Bitterly.*] I was doin' more than chokin' ya. 'N it wasn't yer goddamn asthmer.

[ROSS *moves* COONEY *away, calming him.*]

ROSS: Y'all right now?

COONEY: [*Nodding.*] Uh-huh.

MONKEY: [*To* COONEY.] Goddamn baby.

COONEY: Shut up.

ROSS: Will ya quit it, Monk? Give him a rest.

MONKEY: 'N what're ya Burchett, his momma now?

COONEY: Shut up.

MONKEY: Or maybe he's yer girlfriend, ya rubbin' on him like ya do.

ROSS: What's that supposed ta mean?

MONKEY: Jus' what it does.

ROSS: It's fer his asthmer. I gotta rub his chest a-'cause a' his asthmer.

MONKEY: Don't look that way ta me.

ROSS: Well, that's what it is.

MONKEY: Fine.

ROSS: That's what it is.

MONKEY: I said, "fine."

ROSS: I'm helpin' ya fer yer asthmer, ain't it so, Cooney?

COONEY: Helpin'.

ROSS: Fer yer asthmer.

COONEY: Yeah.

ROSS: See?

> [ROSS *and* COONEY *sit on the tracks. There is a long pause.*]

> Know somethin', Cooney?

COONEY: What?

ROSS: I was thinkin'…ya sure got it rough, all right…first with yer daddy…'n now with yer momma…'n ya bein' an orphan 'n all.

COONEY: Yeah.

ROSS: That's real rough.

COONEY: Buncha friggin' rough.

ROSS: How'd yer momma die? D'ya know?

COONEY: [*Shaking his head in the negative.*] Unh-unh.

ROSS: But it was you found her first when she was, huh?

COONEY: Yup.

ROSS: [*Softly.*] Goddamn.

[*There is a pause.*]

What're ya gonna do?

COONEY: I don't know.

ROSS: Where ya gonna live?

[COONEY *shrugs.*]

MONKEY: [*Turning.*] S' gonna git hisself shunted off ta some foster home somewheres is where. S' gonna git hisself marooned in some ol' home somewheres is where. Somewheres where they could jus' give any ol' care 'bout him. Don't ya go on a-shruggin' yer shoulders, Cooney, 'cause ya know that's jus' what's gonna happen.

COONEY: [*Shaking his head in the negative.*] Unh-unh.

MONKEY: Ya damn sure do.

ROSS: [*To* COONEY.] Yer daddy shouldn't a' messed with Jake Bushey out at McGavick's.

COONEY: He was drinkin'.

MONKEY: [*Crossing.*] He was drunk. I heard about it. Dickie Rembert tol' me 'bout it in the hardware store...how yer daddy went 'n stood outside a' Jake Bushey's callin' him every kind've a no-good bastard 'til Jake finally run him off with a piece a' two by four...'n how yer daddy went home ta git his carvin' knife...then snuck back...caught

Jake 'n dragged him outside the house…dragged him off behind the IGA screamin' louder 'n higher than a stuck pig…'n how he slit his throat. Dickie said how he even turned slow 'n walked on back home ta wait fer the sheriff ta come 'n take him away.

ROSS: He jus' walked back home?

MONKEY: Walked.

ROSS: And waited fer the sheriff ta take him? Didn't even try ta run?

MONKEY: Jus' waited. Right, Cooney?

ROSS: That right?

COONEY: [*Softly.*] Jus' waited. Hunkered down on the porch 'n jus' waited.

MONKEY: Stupid bastard wanted ta git caught. Did it on purpose jus' ta spite ya. Marooned ya right on purpose.

ROSS: [*To* COONEY.] What'd Jake Bushey do ta git him so riled?

COONEY: I don't know.

MONKEY: I do. Jake was a nailin' yer momma. Ain't that right, Cooney?

COONEY: No.

MONKEY: [*Pantomiming with his hips.*] Yer momma 'n ol' Jake were doin' the dirty together, weren't they?

COONEY: Were not.

MONKEY: 'N yer daddy found out. Found out 'n went over ta Jake Bushey's ta git him.

COONEY: [*Standing.*] Ya take that back, Monkey Hill. Ya take that back.

MONKEY: Ya gonna make me?

COONEY: [*Leaping at* MONKEY.] Take it back!

[MONKEY *sidesteps* COONEY *and pushes him to the ground. He straddles him, twisting one of* COONEY'*s arms behind his back.*]

Owwww! Leggo!

ROSS: Git off'a him, Monk.

MONKEY: Say, "My momma 'n Jake Bushey were doin' the dirty."

[ROSS *tries to pry the two apart.*]

ROSS: Git off. He's gonna have his asthmer.

[MONKEY *pushes* ROSS *away.*]

MONKEY: Git yer hands off, Burchett.

[ROSS *tries again to pull* MONKEY *off* COONEY.]

ROSS: He's gonna have his asthmer.

MONKEY: Git off.

[*He throws an elbow at* ROSS, *catching him in the head and throwing him backward to the ground. Then he returns his attention to* COONEY.]

Say, "My momma 'n Jake Bushey were doin' the dirty."

COONEY: Quit it.

MONKEY: Say it first, then I'll quit.

[COONEY *hesitates, refusing to speak.* MONKEY *increases the pressure slightly.*]

Say it.

COONEY: Aaawww!

ROSS: Yer breakin' his arm.

MONKEY: Say it.

ROSS: Yer breakin' his—

MONKEY: Say it.

COONEY: [*Softly.*] My momma 'n Jake Bushey were doin' the dirty.

MONKEY: Louder.

COONEY: [*Louder.*] My momma 'n Jake Bushey were doin' the dirty.

[MONKEY *releases* COONEY *and steps away.*]

MONKEY: See? I told ya.

[COONEY *sits up slowly, massaging and rubbing his arm.*]

It's a sorry thing when a married woman carries on like that. She's a tainted thing. Ain't that right?

COONEY: [*Softly.*] Tainted.

MONKEY: It's a sorry thing ta have a momma who's a whore. I hate ta say it to yer face, Cooney, with her bein' dead 'n all, but that's what she was. A sorry whore.

COONEY: Sorry.

MONKEY: A goddamn dirty rotten shame.

COONEY: Buncha friggin' sorry.

MONKEY: 'N that's how come she's dead too. Went 'n kill't herself jus' like everybody's a-sayin'. Ain't that so?

[*There is a slight pause.*]

ROSS: She kill't herself, Cooney?

COONEY: [*Shaking his head in the negative.*] Unh-unh.

MONKEY: Ain't that so? On account'a Jake Bushey.

ROSS: She really done kill't herself?

COONEY: It was an accident.

MONKEY: She done marooned ya too. See, Cooney?

COONEY: It was an accident.

ROSS: [*Quietly.*] 'N ya was the one found her first.

MONKEY: They done it fer spite. See? Yer momma 'n yer daddy. Marooned ya jus' ta spite ya. Weren't no accident. It ain't never no accident.

[*There is a long pause.* COONEY *looks down at the ground.* ROSS *rubs his head.* MONKEY *looks again toward Manassas.*]

So, hell. Are we gonna go on ta Manassas or what?

[*There is a slight pause.*]

COONEY: [*Settled.*] I ain't goin'.

MONKEY: What'd ya say?

COONEY: I ain't goin'.

MONKEY: Why the hell not?

COONEY: 'Cause I jus' ain't.

MONKEY: Well, Jesus H., that ain't no reason.

ROSS: Maybe we jus' ought'a go back, Monk.

MONKEY: You too, huh Burchett? Yer girlfriend says he ain't gonna—

ROSS: Shut up.

MONKEY: —so you ain't gonna?

ROSS: Why cain't we jus' go on back?

MONKEY: Go back ta what? Ta what? What's me 'n Cooney got ta go back ta?

ROSS: I jus' don't much feel like goin' no more.

MONKEY: Come on.

ROSS: Jus' don't seem right now.

MONKEY: Why the hell not?

ROSS: It jus' don't.

MONKEY: Goddamn.

ROSS: Seems like we already been maybe. Seems now like we been there 'n back. Ain't that right, Cooney? Don't it?

COONEY: I don't know.

ROSS: Like we done been there 'n back.

MONKEY: Y'all ain't been nowhere. Y'ain't been nowhere. It's important. Ain't ya heard nothin' I been tellin' ya? They marooned 'em. They marooned 'em all.

ROSS: I know.

MONKEY: No, ya don't know. Only I know.

[COONEY *steps up on a rail and looks to* ROSS.]

COONEY: I'll balance-race ya back to the crossin'?

MONKEY: What're ya goin' back ta, Cooney?

[ROSS *steps on the other rail.*]

ROSS: [*To* COONEY.] All right.

MONKEY: [*Moving to intercept them.*] Ya ain't leavin'. Neither of ya.

ROSS: Ya ain't gonna make us go, Monk.

MONKEY: I could.

ROSS: I reckon. But you're goin' have ta beat us both good ta do it.

MONKEY: Y'all can come with me. We can run away together.

COONEY: [*Shaking his head in the negative.*] Unh-unh.

MONKEY: Cooney...we gotta see 'em...we gotta see what they done.

COONEY: I ain't goin'.

ROSS: Say "when," Cooney.

MONKEY: Ya need ta go. Cooney, it's you special that's got ta go.

COONEY: "When."

[ROSS *and* COONEY *begin to move off, tottering, walking "tight rope" along the rails.* MONKEY *moves in front, trying to block them.*]

MONKEY: We're kin ta them Confeds. You and me, Cooney. We're kin. Don't ya see? They're orphans too. They was marooned jus' like us. Ya hear what I'm sayin'? Ya hear me, Cooney? Cain't jus' leave.

[COONEY *begins to sing "The Wreck of the Ol' 97" over* MONKEY's *pleas.*]

COONEY: [*Singing.*] "Gave him his orders at Monroe, Virginia, sayin'..."

[ROSS *joins in the song.*]

ROSS and COONEY: "'Engineer you're way behind time...'"

MONKEY: We'll go ta where them Confeds are in Manassas 'n we'll rescue 'em. Come on. We gotta rescue them orphans.

[ROSS *and* COONEY *head off in the direction they came, "tight rope" walking back toward Buckland.*]

ROSS and COONEY: "This ain't the thirty-eight, it's Ol' 97, 'n ya gotta put her in Spencer on time…'"

MONKEY: 'N then we'll go cross that blowed up bridge with 'em…

[*He looks toward Manassas.*]

We'll take 'em across them busted tracks…'n jus' keep on a-goin'.

ROSS and COONEY: "So, he looks roun' ta his coalmen, 'n then at his watch, 'n says 'Boys shovel in some more coal…'"

MONKEY: Jus' keep on them tracks together. Stay on 'em forever 'n not never get off. Be family with 'em. Be family.

[COONEY *and* ROSS *disappear from view, their song slowly fading out. There is a pause.* MONKEY *turns and sees them gone. There is a slight pause as he watches the two move off. Finally, he calls after them.*]

Fine. The hell with ya. I'll do it myself. I'll do it all myself. Who needs ya? Goddamn hell! Who needs any of ya?

[*He picks up their song, singing initially as if to comfort himself, then building to an attack.*]

"She's speedin' down grade on the way inta Danville, when the whistle breaks inta a scream. Train flew off the track 'n was found in a wreck, the men a-scalded ta death by the steam!"

[*He yells off at them.*]

YA HEAR THAT YA BASTARDS? YA HEAR THAT YA NO GOOD BASTARDS? Y'ALL ARE NO BETTER 'N THEM YELLER BASTARD CONFEDS THAT MAROONED MY KIN. Y'ALL ARE NO BETTER THAN MY MOMMA 'N POP THAT

MAROONED ME. YA HEAR THAT COONEY? YA HEAR BURCHETT? YELLER BASTARDS.

[*He turns toward Manassas.*]

YA HEAR THAT GEN'RAL HAUPT? YA HEAR THAT OL' STONEWALL? YA HEAR THAT YA SORRY DEAD CONFED BASTARDS? I'M COMIN' TA GIT YA. I'M MONKEY HILL. I'M MONKEY HILL 'N I'M COMIN' FER YA. YA HEAR ME? YA HEAR ME? YA HEAR ME?

[*No answer comes from the ghosts at Manassas. He looks up at the sun and wipes the sweat from his forehead. He cannot move in either direction. Marooned. Lights fade to black.*]

END OF PLAY

AL TAKES A BRIDE

A Play in One Act

Gary Sunshine

Al Takes a Bride by Gary Sunshine. Copyright © 2002 by Gary Sunshine. All rights reserved. Reprinted by permission of the author.

CAUTION: Professionals and amateurs are hereby warned that *Al Takes a Bride* by Gary Sunshine is subject to a royalty. It is fully protected under the copyright laws of the United States of America, and of all countries covered by the International Copyright Union (including the Dominion of Canada and the rest of the British Commonwealth), and of all countries covered by the Pan-American Copyright Convention and the Universal Copyright Convention, and of all countries with which the United States has reciprocal copyright relations. All rights, including professional, amateur, motion picture, recitation, lecturing, public reading, radio broadcasting, television, video or sound taping, all other forms of mechanical or electronic reproduction, such as information storage and retrieval systems and photo-copyright, and the rights of translation into foreign languages are strictly reserved. Particular emphasis is laid upon the question of readings, permission for which must be secured from the author or his agent in writing.

All inquiries concerning performance rights should be addressed to John B. Santoianni, Abrams Artists Agency, 275 Seventh Avenue, 26th Floor, New York, N.Y. 10001.

Gary Sunshine

GARY SUNSHINE'S play *Mercury* was produced in New York City by HERE Arts Center in association with Eve Ensler (Spring 2001). His work has been seen/developed at New York Theatre Workshop's Just Add Water Festival, MCC Theater, The Flea, the New Group, the Directors Company, the Cherry Lane Alternative, Rising Phoenix Rep, Spectrum Stage, and Manhattan Theater Source. His play *A Tail* was published in *Perfect Ten* (Heinemann), and a monologue from his play *Bigger Than You* was published in *Monologues for Men by Men* (Heinemann). He is currently working as the creator and writer of a documentary about a writing group at a women's maximum security prison. He received an A.B. from Princeton and an M.F.A. from NYU's Dramatic Writing Program, where he was awarded the Harry Kondoleon Graduate Prize for Playwriting and the New York Picture Company Award for Best Dramatic Screenplay.

CHARACTERS:

> ALICE MITCHELL, 19, a formidable and imposing presence, plain but handsomely attractive, quiet with a streak of wild.
> FREDA WARD, 19, a southern belle, meticulously put together, impeccable manners, pleasant as can be.
> JUDGE KETTERSON, 45, intelligent, articulate, full of genteel charm, finely-chiseled features, aging and fading too early.

TIME:

> June 1893. Dusk.

SETTING:

> A riverbank outside of Memphis, Tennessee.

[*At rise, the June sun sets over a riverbank near Memphis. ALICE MITCHELL stands in full, somber skirts, hands on hips, her back to the audience. A large cloth bag, stuffed, sits downstage of her.*]

[*A steamer hoots. ALICE, to calm herself, whips out a flask of whiskey and takes a swig. She coughs hard.*]

[FREDA WARD, *wearing an elaborate, stylish dress, sneaks in just as* ALICE *begins to take another swig.* FREDA *runs up behind* ALICE *and grabs her around the waist.* ALICE *instinctively whirls around and knocks* FREDA *to the ground, screaming:*]

ALICE: I'll kill you before you can breathe!

FREDA: It's me, Al. It's only me. It's your Freddy.

ALICE: Fred? Now what were you doing that for? That's a stupid thing to do—

FREDA: —Wasn't stupid. Just having some fun. Been with my mama all day today—

[FREDA *struggles to get up.*]

ALICE: —Lord, your mama's an old pigface—

FREDA: —and that woman could suck the fun out of a pony ride to the stars. Help me here Alice, come on! Mama never stopped talking from the second we got in the buggy. "The eggs are shamefully tiny this year and Papa's store isn't making good profits this year and however am I going to buy this year's Paris gowns and Jesus lives in Memphis only I can't conjure up his whereabouts: Is Miss Cottonwood hiding our Saviour or is he staying with the Reverend Stanley?" I wouldn't mind if she was just crazy, that'd all be interesting, like your mother, but my mama's just a big bore and my you look particularly lovely today.

[*Silence.* ALICE *stands, transfixed.*]

FREDA: That's sweet, you're having a fit. You know, your fits help me see more of your eyes, all popped open by the awe, the "Mmmmm, Fred's so gorgeous, she jams up my veins and makes me forget how to blink!"

ALICE: I'd blush if I knew how.

FREDA: I'll teach you how to blush. I'll teach you fineness and elegance and all the proper body functions like cooin' and flutterin' and forgetting how to sweat.

ALICE: [*Clearly in on it now.*] No ma'am. I ain't doin' it. Sweatin's my best thing. I'm the best sweater in these here parts and I ain't givin' up my title!

[ALICE *and* FREDA *laugh.* FREDA *grabs* ALICE *by shoulders and kisses her hard.* ALICE *accepts, her hands roaming, hot.* ALICE *suddenly breaks it.*]

FREDA: No Al, please, don't stop me.

ALICE: What time is it?

FREDA: [*Looking at her pocketwatch.*] Seven. Please Al, let me show you how much I—

ALICE: —Didn't feel real—

FREDA: —You embarrassed? Who all's gonna see?

ALICE: Felt like a play kiss.

FREDA: Look, they put us apart 'til the next world takes our souls. So if our being together is an impossibility, we're not really here, right? And if we're not really here, doing naughty things can't be dangerous, right? Naughty badgirl things.

[FREDA *tries to kiss* ALICE.]

ALICE: You just playacting for the squirrels and the trees and the colors. I know the difference.

FREDA: Fine. I'll find a cloud for us and we can kiss there. No, no, then we'd be entertaining the angels, and God might pop in too, so forget it, we'll have to find somewhere else, maybe under the river?

ALICE: You sure they didn't follow you?

FREDA: My mother's stuffing her sides into two or three more dresses before the stores close. I told her I was taking the buggy and I'd meet her by sundown. Why you so jittery?

ALICE: I'm not.

FREDA: It's not your time, is it? You getting one of those awful headaches again?

ALICE: I told you, I'm fine—

FREDA: —Cause I got some powders in the buggy, I just picked them up—

ALICE: Don't you know what tomorrow is?

FREDA: Course I do. Your family's moving to Chattanooga tomorrow. On account of you and me. Our little mess. I know it. But I don't want to think on it right now. Can't we just be here with the river and the air and us and leave the thinking to, I don't know, the goldfish maybe?

[ALICE *laughs.*]

Goldfish think, they do! They have to think because they all look alike. If Mr. Goldfish didn't think, he'd mistake his neighbor goldfish for himself. And that's a dangerous thing to do.

ALICE: I don't know. It could be, I guess.

FREDA: You love me, Al? 'Cause I just adore you.

ALICE: No you don't. You just talking sweet 'cause you think you ain't going to see me again. What time is it?

FREDA: The same time. Now how could you say something so terribly awful like that? I love you now and always will. Not just when you're in Memphis but everywhere, no matter where you'll be.

[*Pause.* FREDA *strokes* ALICE'*s hair.* ALICE *crosses to her bag. She pulls out a man's business suit.*]

FREDA: Whatcha doing now? Oh Al, you brought—

ALICE: —You going to shield me?

FREDA: Well you can't just take off your clothes...

[ALICE *removes her dress.*]

ALICE: Thought we could play, you know, one last time. For now.

[FREDA *hustles to shield* ALICE.]

FREDA: I'd love to play, but my Lord, Alice, how can you just undress like that? What if somebody sees?

ALICE: You're the one who went kiss kiss kiss—

FREDA: —But I am properly covered—

ALICE: —Nobody looks at me, except you.

FREDA: Men'd find you pretty, if you let them. They're just afraid you'll cut their hearts out and hang 'em up on your Christmas tree.

ALICE: I don't really give a damn what they think. You should know that by now.

FREDA: If you ask me, it's a little uncharitable how you act to all those nice men. I am never rude, not to Willie Watkins or Jimmie Lynn or Ashley Roselle—

ALICE: —Specially not to Ashley.

FREDA: Well, Ashley's the nicest of all. You'd like Ashley too, if you gave him half a chance.

ALICE: I'm sure I would. Here, help me with this.

FREDA: He asks me sometimes, he says "Miss Freda, tell me, am I such a low-down dirty dog that I don't even deserve a 'Mornin!' from Miss Alice?" And all I can say to Ashley is... wait Al. I know this suit.

ALICE: It's my Daddy's.

FREDA: Isn't it the one he was wearing when he lost Mr. Kiley to the Malone's carriage? Still got a little of Mr. Kiley's blood on it, see?

ALICE: He never wears it anymore. Whenever he loses a patient who ain't old, Daddy takes off his suit soon as he gets home and never puts it on again. Fits me snug, must say.

FREDA: Don't matter how it fits you, Al. It's got death on its sleeve.

ALICE: It's all dried up, silly. Death's wet, not dry. Dry means it's over with. Straighten up my collar? There. I look good, don't you think?

[FREDA *studies* ALICE.]

Want to make more of a fellow outta me?

FREDA: How's that, Al? Or should I say Alvin.

ALICE: Take your pick.

[ALICE *whips out a shaving brush, cup and a straight razor.*]

FREDA: Oh Al, this ole thing scares me to no end!

ALICE: I'll get the lather going.

FREDA: I'm not so good at it.

ALICE: Every good wife grooms her man. That's her privilege. Now, let's go, and watch my nose, I only got one.

FREDA: If we're just playing, Al, we can make up the rules ourselves. And I say no shaving. It's too dark here.

ALICE: If you want to play at Bride 'n Groom, you shave me. If you been lying to me all this time, you're not interested in being by my side, then leave the razor be and please get out of my sight.

[*Short pause.*]

FREDA: Oh Al, you're such a dramatic one. Course I'll shave you. But don't you come crying to me if I make your blood go sputting—

ALICE: [*Stern, a little menacing.*] —Not a nick.

[ALICE *sits on a stump.* FREDA *carefully starts to shave* ALICE's "mustache."]

ALICE: A man don't like to be shaved in silence. Makes him suspicious. Like the barber's got thoughts.

FREDA: Well Al, what should I say? I woke up at half past seven and Everett was making the most dreadful banging up and down the stairs, I swear it was a terrible mistake to get that little boy a drum, but after the Easter parade, it was all he could talk about—

ALICE: Sing, Fred. Don't babble. Sing for me.

[*Beat.*]

FREDA: No. The way he admired that drum corps last Easter, what else could I get him for his birthday? And he has been such a good little brother, such a comfort ever since mama and daddy found out about you and me, Al—

ALICE: —I said sing!!!!

FREDA: [*Angry, very shrill and dissonant.*]
La la la la la la
La do do la do do do deee—

ALICE: [*Soft.*] Please. It's *my* comfort.

[FREDA *stops, approaches the stump and resumes the shave while humming a beautiful Irish lullaby. When she finishes shaving:*]

ALICE: What time is it, Fred?

FREDA: A shave and a kiss later. Why you so interested in the time?

ALICE: Not a lot of time left, that's all. Now walk a few paces and tell me if you can see it, under my nose.

FREDA: Stubble takes a while on a real man.

ALICE: I know, but maybe it started already. Go on.

FREDA: We can just pretend it's there, Al. That's the beauty of pretending. Things are only as real as you want them to be. You don't need an honest mustache, just one you see in your head.

ALICE: I've shaved it three times this week. Swear it's going to come in fuller than the Senator's.

FREDA: I don't have feelings for the Senator.

ALICE: 'Cause why?

FREDA: 'Cause why. 'Cause he's not my Al, that's why. Can't you make your family stay in Memphis forever? Then at least we could go on like this, indefinitely. We'd have our times, plain and simple. Wouldn't matter what else happened in our lives, what we did or who we did it with, we could always come back to each other, here by the river under the moon, or before the day—

ALICE: —Our times is when its dark out?

[*Short beat.*]

FREDA: And even if I was to marry—

ALICE: —Marry???—

FREDA: —Or get in some sort of permanent—

ALICE: —Who you marrying, Fred?—

FREDA: —situation, or you, you maybe could—

ALICE: —Ashley, that fat faced demon—

FREDA: —You, you could get swept off your feet—

ALICE: —Tell me, it's Ashley—

FREDA: —Not what I'm talking about, Alice. All I'm saying—

ALICE: —I want to play some more—

FREDA: —Is that if you want something bad enough, you got to figure out how to give in a little. Compromise. Now it's too late. Your parents carting you off cause you let them believe the truth about us. You let them just swipe our truth from your hands, you gave it to them, 'stead of protecting it.

ALICE: I brought you something, Fred.

[ALICE *crosses to her bag and pulls out a wedding dress.*]

FREDA: It's gorgeous! It's the most gorgeous old thing I ever seen!

ALICE: You think it's too old?

FREDA: No, it's just heaven!

ALICE: Cause it is old. It was my mama's. Put it on. See what it makes you into.

FREDA: What if I soil it? No, I'll gaze at it, marvel at all the little beads and fine lace, and I'll imagine it on me.

[*Pause.*]

Oh, *Gawwwd*, I'm putting it on!!!

[FREDA *starts to take off her dress, then stops.*]

FREDA: It's indecent. Do something, cover me!

[*Pause.* ALICE *covers* FREDA *manically, circling her fast, like a rain dance.*]

FREDA: That's positively savage. Just stand in front of me and keep a sharp eye's all.

[FREDA *changes quickly as* ALICE *watches for others, occasionally peeking at* FREDA, *who speaks the following while changing:*]

Now a dress like this cannot be worn by any old one. You, Al, perfect as you may be, could not do this dress justice. Wouldn't work, no ma'am. Cause you don't believe in it. You don't believe in finery, but you appreciate it on me. Oh, if only I had a mirror. Oh, did I get caught there, no. Al, do up the back, do it up!

[ALICE *crosses and adjusts* FREDA's *dress.*]

I can see myself in this beautiful dress, my face as white as lillies, my hair a sunburst beaming down to my train, my waist a tiny halo, sculpted upward toward my softness, wrapped tight and secure, peeking out to my chin, which has never stood prouder, never lovelier. And

I am this dress, exquisite and artful, the most pleasing memory ever formed... and you think I'm a loon.

ALICE: Brides can't help being stuck up. The dress gets into their skin.

FREDA: Oh, but Al. I feel perfectly divine and strong. Now where's the veil?

ALICE: I'm sorry. I couldn't find it.

FREDA: [*Very upset.*] I would never, ever get married without a veil! It's practically in the Bible, Thy bride shalt wear a veil, oh you don't know it because you're something of a heathen. The wedding's called off. I'm incomplete!

ALICE: You're much too beautiful to hide behind a veil.

[*Pause.*]

FREDA: Do I have the beauty of an angel or a statue? Should I fly to the heavens or stand perfectly still?

ALICE: Say what you always say about a Memphis wedding. I love the words you got for it.

FREDA: What? Oh! In a Memphis wedding, the bride and groom walk down the aisle sweeter than in any other city in the world.

ALICE: The other part!

FREDA: And the minister says his sermon, and they exchange vows, and just before they kiss, right here in Memphis, they're supposed to feel God's Divine right hand pushing the smalls of their backs. If the couple can feel His Divine right hand, they know they're truly blessed. The pressure of God's hand pushes them together, and their lips lock in a holy partnership, protected from all bad, all sadnesses, for a long, long time to come.

ALICE: And God knows to show up?

FREDA: 'Course he does. That's why there's a ceremony. So he can mark "Memphis wedding" on his calendar weeks in advance.

[ALICE *crosses away from* FREDA *and then starts to march slowly back to her, a procession.*]

And what's more is they say the bride can see a reflection of God's right hand in the eyes of all her guests. In the eyes of the whole town.

ALICE: No guests, but we're still in Memphis.

FREDA: You really want to play the whole thing through? You are too precious!

ALICE: I know how important it is to you. A Memphis ceremony.

[*Short pause.*]

"We are so blessed. Thanks to y'all for showing up. We're celebrating this blessed union." Where you want us to be, Fred? The church?

FREDA: No. How about we pretend we're right here, right where we are?

ALICE: Will God find us?

FREDA: He's probably very busy this evening. Let's leave him be.

ALICE: I want God here for you!

[*Beat.*]

OK, let's get on with it. "Do you Freda Ward, take—"

FREDA: —Al, can't you say something pretty first? A wedding should be blooming with pretty words, smart things for the couple to take with them down the long, long road of married life.

ALICE: You want inspiration?

FREDA: Yes, I guess you could call it that.

ALICE: Well, I'm inspired, but not in a speaking way.

FREDA: "A couple brought together in the name of love—"

ALICE: —"Here in Memphis"—

FREDA: "—is the most sacred thing you can find in the world."

ALICE: Amen. "Do you Freda P. Ward—"

FREDA: "Bonded by honor and duty, they take their steps together, one by one, their breaths braid, their eyes see the same visions. One protects while the other soothes, one provides while the other feeds, and together they shall multiply."

ALICE: Multiply? Lord Fred, I don't know about that—

FREDA: "—and increase their love by tenfold. A hundredfold. Forever and ever."

[*Pause.*]

ALICE: [*With great sincerity.*] I take you for my own, Freda Ward. To love and honor and I'll protect you from everything rotten. I don't care who hates us because I love you. And I'll put food on your table and buy you French dresses and be nice to your friends when you give them tea and cookies. And I'll always, always trust you, never call you a liar for a second.

FREDA: Course not. I'd never lie. Told you that!

ALICE: Can you feel it yet?

FREDA: Feel what?

ALICE: God's right hand? I think I feel it just about... here.

FREDA: No, I don't feel it.

ALICE: Tell me you want to feel it, Freda. Please.

FREDA: If I could. If I could choose my life.

[ALICE *kisses* FREDA, *with great tenderness and passion.*]

ALICE: Is your heart made of leather, Fred? Tough leather that can last through it all?

FREDA: I love you, Al.

ALICE: I see things, Fred. A future—

FREDA: —It's what I know.

ALICE: There's a way to what we both got to have...

[JUDGE KETTERSON *enters.*]

KETTERSON: What a remarkable vision.

[FREDA *catches* JUDGE KETTERSON *out of the corner of her eye and shrieks.*]

FREDA: Leave us alone!

ALICE: What the hell took you so long?

FREDA: She and I steal five minutes together and the whole town come after us? Please, let us be.

[*Steamer hoots.*]

ALICE: Lord, what time is it?

FREDA: Oh, get a watch of your own!

KETTERSON: Don't fret, Miss Mitchell. I'm here, just as I promised.

FREDA: You invited him here?

ALICE: I made a way, Fred. For us to be together.

FREDA: [*Looking at* KETTERSON.] Now, Alice, the whole town knows you Mitchells are up and moving tomorrow, right Judge?

ALICE: I'm not going.

FREDA: What?

KETTERSON: She's not going there... she's got other plans. Haven't you told her, Miss... Mr... Miss Mitchell?

[*Steamer hoots again.*]

ALICE: Oh damn. Get them papers out, Judge, now!

FREDA: Shhhh! Stop your fooling. Now, course she's going, she's got no choice.

ALICE: I got choices. Plenty. So do you, if you'd stop and think on it.

FREDA: It's cast in stone, Al. Your mama and daddy's made up their minds, they've got to follow it through, told my folks and everything. They feel it's their duty to save you—

KETTERSON: You look quite lovely, Miss Ward. Ravishing. Why, I could court a girl like you.

ALICE: *Hah!*

FREDA: Judge Ketterson, I ought to let you know that Mama's planning a sweet dinner for you and your sister sometime this month—

ALICE: —Don't go social on me—

FREDA: —maybe make some of her chicken pies?

KETTERSON: No better pies in Memphis!

FREDA: She just has to set the date, but thought I'd give you nice warning so you can find an empty space on y'all's calendar for us.

ALICE: [*To* KETTERSON:] Didn't tell you to talk friendly.

KETTERSON: No, ma'am. I apologize.

ALICE: Now Fred, darling. You was saying what to me? Before he got here.

[*Beat.*]

I'm sorry, I can't quite make it out. Say it again?

FREDA: I don't recall.

ALICE: Hunh. That's hard for me to believe. Let me help you. It started with I love you, Al. Judge wants to hear. Go on. He knows all about it.

FREDA: Everyone's heard those silly rumors—

ALICE: —The truth. He knows the truth. Ain't he sweet? Sweet li'l snake! So say it Fred.

[*Beat.*]

Unless it ain't true. Unless you don't love me. Unless you never loved me.

FREDA: I love you, Al. I love her, Judge. Isn't she the most lovable thing?

KETTERSON: Yes, I'd say so, but what kind of judge am—

ALICE: —For real, Fred.

FREDA: Alice—

ALICE: —Not play. For real. Please.

[*Pause.*]

FREDA: I love you, Al.

ALICE: Now then! Judge, I do believe you got work to do.

[KETTERSON *turns to his satchel and pulls out some papers and a book.* ALICE *moves* FREDA *to the perfect position.*]

FREDA: What? What is this?

ALICE: Judge's helping us out. He agreed to it and that makes me so, so grateful.

FREDA: Agreed to what, Al?

KETTERSON: I hope I remembered all my materials.

ALICE: Fred. If it was a possible thing—

KETTERSON: —Where's my robe?—

FREDA: —Agreed to what?—

ALICE: —A possible thing! If it could be made real and not playing, would you want us to be put together forever?

KETTERSON: I don't feel like a judge without my robe.

ALICE: Judge—

KETTERSON: —My robe was stained, and I thought our girl cleaned it and placed it in my bag. This is awfully embarrassing, Miss Mitchell, awfully embarrassing.

FREDA: Please go now, Judge.

KETTERSON: I cannot.

FREDA: With all the sweetest respect, we were having a very important and very private visit.

ALICE: He's marrying us, Fred. With or without the damn robe.

FREDA: That's the silliest thing I ever heard.

ALICE: Show her. Now.

[KETTERSON *presents* FREDA *with a document.*]

KETTERSON: Formal contract of marriage between one Miss Freda P. Ward and... Mr. Alvin Mitchell.

FREDA: I don't believe it.

KETTERSON: All I need is two willing parties.

[*Short beat.*]

ALICE: He can do it, Fred, he can do it for us. He'll marry us, as long as we go away and never come back. Just like we said before—

FREDA: —When, we never said it—

ALICE: —Course we did, many times—

FREDA: —Never, never did we say—

ALICE: —We played it in your room, downstairs in your daddy's store, in the attic over the church, here—

FREDA: —Just playing, not for real! My God, Alice. Leave here?

[*Beat.*]

Where would we go?

ALICE: St. Louis first. The packer's setting off at eight. Then to New Orleans. That's why I keep asking you about the time. I got tickets and everything.

[*She takes them out and shows them to* FREDA.]

FREDA: And how're we going to live, Al, betcha didn't think for a second about that.

ALICE: I'll be Alvin Mitchell, that's why I'm aiming for that mustache.

[KETTERSON *giggles, then covers it up.*]

If I'm a man, I can get work doing all sorts of things. Start small, maybe a clerk for the railroad, maybe working with my hands, I'm good with tools. Maybe even become a doctor like my daddy.

KETTERSON: Why not become a judge? Or the president? I'm sure you'll pose quite a threat to the Cleveland administration.

ALICE: Quiet!

[*Short pause.*]

We'll get a little spot to live in New Orleans, boarding house maybe, cheap to let, but you'll make it so homey that we won't never be ashamed to bring on the people! Every Saturday night we'll make dinner for lots of friends, different than the kind we got here, the kind you got. These friends'd laugh their hearts out at Memphis, cause they maybe came from places just like it... that's what we'll do on Saturday nights, we'll be laughing, you can sing, maybe we'll get a piano—

FREDA: —Why you here Judge, sir. How'd she get you to come?

KETTERSON: I've known Miss Mitchell since she was so tiny... and sweet. An obligation of friendship.

FREDA: Whatchu do to him, Alice? Tell the truth. You threaten him, your usual way?

ALICE: No, not threaten him. Just kind of entered into, how'd you say it, Judge, an agreement.

KETTERSON: If y'all are about ready... I have numbness up and down my legs, sometimes all over my body. Comes and goes.

FREDA: I can't imagine what you and the judge would possibly agree on. Is it shady, Al? That'd be just like you, putting my name into something shady, then going off to Chattanooga and leaving me with my reputation all besmirched.

ALICE: I'm not leaving you, Fred! Don't you follow? We're leaving together.

KETTERSON: Miss Mitchell, I am perfectly prepared to carry out your wishes. Perfectly prepared. But I would like to voice my faint suspicion—

ALICE: —Your suspicions ain't worth my spit. Just your papers and your signature, thank you kindly.

FREDA: What's your suspicion, Judge?

KETTERSON: Far be it for me to interfere—

ALICE: —He don't have no right to even be a judge, he pretends he's for one thing but then does something else behind the doors, he's a scandal waiting to happen.

KETTERSON: It seems that, perhaps... Miss Ward is somewhat confused. Her mind is swirling, all the excitement. Am I correct in assuming so, Miss Ward?

FREDA: Perhaps... somewhat. What scandal, Al?

KETTERSON: Do you doubt your beauty, Miss Freda?

FREDA: No sir, I do not. What scandal, Al?

KETTERSON: Do you fear that no one listens to you?

FREDA: Al listens, so does my brother, a few of my other girlfriends. What scandal, Al?

ALICE: There's not even whispers about him yet, Fred, but there could be. I just have to strike the match and poof, he'll have flames all around him.

KETTERSON: My! What a fantastic imagination she has!

ALICE: I spotted him with fellas, Fred.

FREDA: Fellas?

ALICE: One or two we went to school with—

KETTERSON: —Imagination is a wonderful gift. But gifts can go bad—

ALICE: —Very familiar faces, Fred, you'd be amazed!—

KETTERSON: —in diseased minds, the imagination becomes destructive... It's bound to happen, Miss Ward, it's proven in the medical literature.

FREDA: Can't be. He's the judge. You were seeing funny, Al.

ALICE: Oh, I saw him all right. Spied on him through his back porch. All groping and kissing and—

KETTERSON: —I've seen it in my courtroom, Miss Ward. First the paranoia—

ALICE: —Judge messes up the fella's hair first—

KETTERSON: —then the delusions, then the violent outbursts, the threats and scheming, finally, unless stopped—

ALICE: —He strokes the fella's face—

KETTERSON: —a criminal mind fully formed, prone to violent deviant acts—

ALICE: —Then he rips off the fella's shirt—

KETTERSON: —against the ones closest to her, Miss Ward—

ALICE: —and licks the fella's chest all over—

KETTERSON: —You're scared she's going to do you harm—

ALICE: —Course she ain't. I'd never—

KETTERSON: —You're scared she'll destroy you!

[FREDA *slaps* KETTERSON. *Beat, then:*]

ALICE: Marry me, Fred. It's possible. Marry me now.

KETTERSON: Young lady gets to wear a wedding gown only once. Don't you think you should wait for that perfect day, when you've found your life's mate, Miss Ward?

ALICE: That's me, she's found me, isn't that right Fred?

KETTERSON: You're a lovely girl, with excellent breeding, good manners, and, if I may say, a fine way of pleasing the eye, Miss Ward, very fine indeed. A treasure for the most noble, goodhearted husband. One as beautiful as you.

ALICE: Judge'll dream you up your perfect beau, but then he'll run off with the fellow himself. Stop listening to him—

FREDA: —Alice! Stop. Please.

[*Beat.*]

Judge. Do you do... things... with fellas?

KETTERSON: Your perfect beau... your perfect life... will find you, Miss Ward. Maybe he already has.

FREDA: Stop treating me like a girl in a story. Tell me. Do you do what Al said you do?

ALICE: Course he does, he's like us—

FREDA: —I'm not asking you, Al. Tell me, Judge. Do you... have relations with fellas? Like Alice and me?

KETTERSON: Beauty seeks beauty.

ALICE: [*Muttering*] Bunk. I seek Fred. Judge seeks fellas. Period.

KETTERSON: Goodness can only acquire the face of perfection, Miss Ward—

ALICE: —Do you see it now, Fred?

KETTERSON: —It lights the faces of you and the handsome boy who will someday be your groom. Your perfect beau—

ALICE: —He can't say who he loves, not even out here under the moon, not even into the river... watch this, watch.

[ALICE *drags* KETTERSON *to the river and pushes his head downward.*]

Can you tell the water the truth, Judge?

FREDA: You'll crack his back, Al!

ALICE: Can you tell the fish? Go on, tell the fish... I like fellas, fishies, I kiss fellas, fishies, I touch fellas—

KETTERSON: —Through beauty, goodness draws attention to itself, to make sure you and your perfect beau find each other and form a fair and righteous union. So you can feel God's right hand, pushing you together—

FREDA: —God's right hand! Tell me the truth, Judge, I won't spread it—

KETTERSON: —If Miss Mitchell here starts in with her lies about either of us, well, we could be each other's witness, each attesting to the other's truth.

FREDA: What truth?

KETTERSON: You are so... lovely! You deserve such a lovely life. We all do.

[*Long pause.*]

FREDA: So Al is right about you?

KETTERSON: No one knows better than I what you must do to survive.

FREDA: And be happy?

ALICE: [*Softly*] Marry me, Fred. Now, right here. The Memphis ceremony you dream about.

FREDA: [*To* KETTERSON:] And be happy?

[*Beat.*]

You sad man.

ALICE: Let's not be sad, Fred. Marry me. See the future. See what I see.

FREDA: Show me, Al. Show me again.

ALICE: Pretty pictures that breathe, Fred. Pictures of two women. Sleeping on the bed they made together out of walnut. Moon's peeking through the window onto the sheets, see it? Soft linens, not scratchy, but soft like the wind. It's quiet, except for the air moving in and out of the women's mouths.

FREDA: It's us.

KETTERSON: Your friend will search and wander.

ALICE: It could be us.

KETTERSON: By the end of it all, when her heart has shriveled, maybe she'll even find her place. Maybe that's how it ends.

FREDA: But you don't know for sure.

ALICE: In my heart—

FREDA: —No! Not your damned heart! I need evidence. Proof that things go that way, someplace. New Orleans. Proof.

[*Pause.*]

KETTERSON: If you have any choice, please, Miss Ward... please choose a softer life. Over in town, I'm sure there's a perfect beau, waiting to protect you.

ALICE: But I'll protect you. I'll always—

FREDA: —If I should happen to miss my perfect beau, should he come to me and I look away, for one reason or another—

KETTERSON: —Nineteen years ago, what did your papa and mama dream for their little girl? And you, did you dream you'd someday grow to be a beautiful woman, the belle of all Memphis, or a shadow? If you miss your perfect beau, you might very well disappear, with only the whispers of others to feed your lungs. Imagine, breathing other people's whispers for the rest of your life! Take what's rightfully yours, Miss Ward. Take it!

[KETTERSON *extends his hand to* FREDA, *as if to take her away. In fear, in a trance, she starts to fall into him.* ALICE *lurches to break them up.*]

ALICE: Let go of her!

FREDA: I don't want to disappear!

KETTERSON: You were meant to walk in the light of Memphis. Not in the shadows.

ALICE: I'm going to the newspaper, judge. I'm going to the Reverend Stanley. Everyone's gonna hear—

FREDA: —No. No one will hear a thing. I'll see to it.

KETTERSON: Thank you, Miss Ward. I'll always remember your kindness. Let me lead you back to the road.

FREDA: I can take care of myself now, thank you.

[KETTERSON *crosses to leave, hurriedly. Steamer hoots.* ALICE *catches him.*]

ALICE: You got to marry us—

KETTERSON: —She won't have you.

FREDA: Let him go, Al.

ALICE: We had a deal—

KETTERSON: —And even if she did, it wouldn't be for long.

[*Smiling, kindly:*]

She's not like you, Miss Mitchell. Neither of us is.

[KETTERSON *exits.* ALICE *and* FREDA *stand looking at each other.* FREDA, *scared and ashamed, gazes away and begins to unbutton the back of her dress:*]

FREDA: I'm just going to take this beautiful gown off right about now. Save it for another time.

[ALICE *grabs her by the arm and squeezes in silence.*]

FREDA: You're hurting me.

[*Pause.*]

I can't feel my fingers, Al.

[*Pause.*]

I can't feel my fingers!

ALICE: He's weak.

[*Releasing* FREDA's *wrist:*]

You are not weak. Not us. Not me.

FREDA: He's sad. And you are not to do him any harm. You understand me?

[*Short beat.*]

Shield me while I take this off.

ALICE: Keep it on.

FREDA: I can't go back into town like this.

ALICE: You're going to marry me now, Fred. You're scared but that's fine because I told you over and over, I'll protect you, that's why I'm wearing the suit.

FREDA: I want to take this dirty old dress off! Now!!!

[ALICE *crosses to* FREDA *and tears the dress off her.* FREDA *remains standing. Silence.*]

ALICE: There. You're free now.

[FREDA *begins to remove the rest of her dress, then puts on her regular clothes.*]

FREDA: I know you're angry. Wedding breaks down right in front of your eyes, you've got good reason to hate me and everybody else in the world. And it's not that I don't appreciate your planning, I do, I swear, it's the sweetest thing I ever heard and I wish, I so do wish I could accommodate you. But I can't. And that's all.

ALICE: I understand.

FREDA: You do? You truly do?

[*She hugs* ALICE, *and sits her down next to her.*]

My Lord, that's a relief. 'Cause I'd hate to be a bad spot in your thoughts, specially when, for a while, that's the only place you'll see me, in your thoughts.

ALICE: It's hard. For us. People and all. Too hard.

FREDA: And that's awful cruel, isn't it? Love's love, that's what I believe. But the world, I just don't know about it. There, think I'm back together now.

ALICE: You love anybody, Freda?

FREDA: [*Not getting it.*] Course I do. I love you, Al, and I always will. Not just when you're in Memphis—

ALICE: —You love anybody, Freda?

FREDA: Yes, Al, but—

ALICE: —You love anybody, Freda?

[*Silence.*]

FREDA: Person's got to know herself. Got to know what she's capable of before she ups and puts herself in situations beyond her capacities.

ALICE: But how do you know—

FREDA: —Every animal figures out what it needs, Al. The beauteous air tempts Missy Goldfish, but she stays down below in the dark, and takes the oxygen from the water, like she's supposed to.

ALICE: Wait 'til some man feeds her his worm.

FREDA: I was meant to walk in the lights of Memphis, Al. Loved and cared for. Walking down an aisle carrying wildflowers or roses, proud of who I grew up to be, proud of who I'm marrying because the world is admiring us... you can't understand because it never crosses your mind Al, it's not part of you, and that's fine, it really is fine for you. But I cannot imagine anything else for me.

ALICE: You marrying anybody Freda?

FREDA: I'd marry you Al, but like you said, it's just too hard.

ALICE: You marrying anybody, Freda?

FREDA: Stop it, Al.

ALICE: Are you marrying anybody Freda? Are. You. Marrying. Anybody. Freda?

FREDA: [*Screaming.*] Ashley Roselle!

[*Pause. With great calm:*]

Ashley Roselle asked me to marry him, and I've accepted his proposal.

ALICE: Hunh.

[ALICE *begins to clean up, putting things back into her bag, but leaving the razor for last. She pauses, looks up:*]

Ashley. Hunh.

[*Silence.* ALICE *continues to clean up.*]

FREDA: My folks are giving me a second chance. I've decided to take it is all. I wanted to tell you right away, I tell you absolutely everything, but you've always been so edgy when it comes to Ashley, and what with your going away, I thought I'd write it in a letter.

ALICE: A letter. Hunh.

FREDA: Wish you'd stop doing your "hunhs," Al. Not just now but always. It's so ungainly.

ALICE: Ungainly? Hunh.

FREDA: He asked me several times, at the church social last month, at the Lyceum a few weeks back, even once in the middle of the night, he threw pebbles at my bedroom window, then Daddy spotted him, and Ashley run like wild, thought my daddy'd shoot him like an old dog! Ashley wore me down.

[ALICE *picks up the razor.*]

ALICE: Funny, if I was a man, I don't think I'd ever shave off my whiskers. I'd let the hair grow.

FREDA: [*Laughing too fast.*] Wonder what color your beard'd be?

ALICE: Let it grow til it reached the ground. Nobody'd say nothing to me about it. Not a word.

[ALICE *opens razor and, at first, gently brushes it across her neck, from the bottom up.*]

FREDA: Sweet Jesus, what are you doing Al?

ALICE: Grooming.

FREDA: Oh. But you don't have any... Alice!!! You're cut!

[ALICE *has drawn blood on her neck and up toward her chin.*]

ALICE: My blood's cold. Just like they say.

FREDA: [*Racing over to stop her.*] Don't kill yourself Alice! Not over me!

[FREDA *tries to grab razor away from* ALICE. ALICE *gets her in a headlock and holds the razor to* FREDA's *throat.*]

ALICE: Can you feel God's right hand now, Fred?

FREDA: Yes, Al. I feel it!

ALICE: Can't live in this world if you're with somebody else. Wouldn't be able to think, Fred, think smart things like how the fish are and "Don't kill yourself, Alice!" Can't live here if I know your best thoughts are going to somebody else.

FREDA: —Judge'll hear my hollering—

ALICE: —Shoulda cut him first. Cut his tongue out too. Belongs in a jackal's mouth.

FREDA: You stopped loving me, is that it? If that's so, then kill me, do it now, I'd like that.

[ALICE *moves to cut* FREDA, *but stops herself.*]

FREDA: Or are you too selfish to love me entirely, in the real world and all? I thought more of you, Al. Thought you had strength of character. Thought you gave freely to what you cared most about. If you changed that much, then maybe the world's gone dark. And I shouldn't live in it. If that's so, then kill me, do it now.

ALICE: You, you lied—

FREDA: —But if you got a ounce of feeling in you, a ounce of what I feel for you, then you'll—

[ALICE *drops* FREDA *to the ground.* FREDA *sobs for a second, then recovers, pulls herself up, gathers her belongings, starts to leave, then looks at* ALICE, *who has crumpled to the ground.* FREDA *takes out a handkerchief, crosses to* ALICE, *and starts to wipe her neck.* ALICE *fights back screams of pain.*]

FREDA: Brave. Like a—

ALICE: [*Finally starts to sob.*] —You can't leave me. You can't leave me.

FREDA: Got to. Got to have my life. And you got to have yours.

ALICE: But where? Where is my life, Fred. You going to throw me in jail? 'S that where my life is?

FREDA: You deserve it! No, course not silly. You just got shocked. I never know how to spring good news on anyone. That's why they print the announcement in the papers. So the bride doesn't have to go round surprising everyone! That must sting, you got to get to your daddy.

ALICE: [*Defiant.*] No ma'am. I am not—

FREDA: —Tell him you walked into a brier patch. Tell him you lost your way.

[FREDA *rises to leave.*]

ALICE: Where is it, Al? Where is my life if Ashley's gone and taken it away from me? And don't tell me in Chattanooga with Mama and Papa.

FREDA: Not there, Al, I know that now.

ALICE: Then where? Under the water with the goldfish? Up on a cloud? Where?

FREDA: Don't know for sure. New Orleans maybe? Wherever, it's away from here. Someplace different... far away, of course. Where the women lie next to each other on walnut beds, snoring! Snoring loud and together.

ALICE: And you don't want that? How could you not want that?

FREDA: If anybody knows where to look for that place, it's you. 'Cause you got no other choice.

ALICE: You got choices? Inside you?

FREDA: The other place, that's where your air is. I believe I can breathe in Memphis with Ashley—

ALICE: —And if you can't?

FREDA: I'll learn. Real fast. Walking down that aisle. Wearing that dress. Orchids. Ashley's arm. The town looking on us, gazing, joyful, I am in their joy, learning by the second...

[*Pause. FREDA snaps out of it and finally is ready to leave.*]

Goodbye Al, my only Al.

[FREDA *exits.* ALICE *takes out her flask, takes a swig, then sits, day giving way to moonlight.*]

[*Pause.*]

[ALICE *slowly pulls out the razor and opens it. She gazes off in the direction* FREDA *has just exited. She rises.*]

[*Lights bump to black.*]

END OF PLAY

RELATIVE STRANGERS

Sheri Wilner

Relative Strangers by Sheri Wilner Copyright © 2001 by Sheri Wilner. All Rights Reserved.

CAUTION: Professionals and amateurs are hereby warned that performance of *Relative Strangers* is subject to a royalty. It is fully protected under the copyright laws of the United States of America, and of all countries covered by the International Copyright Union (including the Dominion of Canada and the rest of the British Commonwealth), and of all countries covered by the Pan-American Copyright Convention and the Universal Copyright Convention, the Berne Convention and of all countries with which the United States has reciprocal copyright relations. All rights, including professional/amateur stage rights, motion picture, recitation, lecturing, public reading, radio broadcasting, television, video or sound recording, all other forms of mechanical or electronic reproduction, such as CD-ROM, CD-I, information storage and retrieval systems and photocopying, and the rights of translation into foreign languages, are strictly reserved. Particular emphasis is placed upon the matter of readings, permission for which must be secured from the Author's agent in writing.

Inquiries concerning all other rights should be addressed to Mary Harden, Harden-Curtis Associates, 850 Seventh Avenue, Suite 903, New York, NY 10019

Sheri Wilner

SHERI WILNER received her M.F.A. in Playwriting from Columbia University in 1999. Her play *Relative Strangers* has been produced at New Georges (New York City), the Organic Theater Company (Chicago), the 2001 Boston Women on Top Festival, and the Pittsburgh New Works Festival. Her other plays include: *Bake Off*, co-recipient of the 2001 Heideman Award and produced at the Actor's Theatre of Louisville's 2002 Humana Festival; *Labor Day*, co-recipient of the 1998 Heideman Award and produced at ATL's 1999 Humana Festival; *Hunger*, produced by the Contemporary American Theatre Festival in Shepherdstown, WV; *Joan of Arkansas*, produced at ATL, New York Performance Works, and New Georges; *Little Death of a Salesman*, produced at the 2000 Boston Women On Top Festival; and her most recent work, *Father Joy*. All of her plays have been published in numerous anthologies, including *Hunger* in *New Playwrights: The Best New Plays of 1999* (Smith & Kraus). She lives in New York City and was named a 2000-1 Dramatists Guild Playwriting Fellow.

CHARACTERS:

MARIE BARRETT, 25 years old.
MARIE HARVEY, 49 years old.
VIRGINIA, 35-45 years old. Head flight attendant. Speaks with a
Southern accent.

SETTING:

On board an airplane flying from New York City to Charleston,
South Carolina.

TIME:

Present day.

[*The voice of an airline pilot can be heard over the intercom.*]

VOICE OF PILOT: Once again, ladies and gentlemen, from the flight
deck, it's our pleasure to welcome you aboard National Airlines Flight
1738 from New York City to Charleston, South Carolina. Flight time
is approximately one hour and forty-four minutes, which means we
should be landing at 12:44 P.M.

[*Lights gradually rise to reveal two women seated next to each other in an
airplane. It is a few minutes after take-off. MARIE BARRETT, seated
on the aisle, reads a book without the overhead light on. MARIE HARVEY,
seated by the window, reads a magazine. She appears uncomfortable and fre-
quently looks at MARIE BARRETT.*]

I'd like to take this opportunity to thank you for selecting National
Airlines. We bring people together.

MARIE HARVEY: You cram people together.

MARIE BARRETT: I'm sorry. Am I crowding you? Here, I'll move
my jacket.

MARIE HARVEY: They really pile us on top of each other…

[*Indicates seat belt.*]

… and strap us down. If they truly wanted to "ensure our comfort," they wouldn't strap us down.

MARIE BARRETT: Don't they have to? For safety's sake?

MARIE HARVEY: Do you feel safe bound up like a prisoner? I sure as hell don't.

MARIE BARRETT: Planes scare me no matter what.

[MARIE HARVEY *returns to her magazine. She is not interested in conversation, but tries to remain polite.*]

MARIE HARVEY: Don't worry. You're safer up here than you are down there.

MARIE BARRETT: Do you live in New York?

MARIE HARVEY: I live about an hour's drive from Manhattan. Twenty minutes if you walk.

MARIE BARRETT: I've only lived there for three years. I'm originally from Rhode Island.

MARIE HARVEY: Quite a change.

MARIE BARRETT: Yeah, it was. The biggest I've made.

MARIE HARVEY: There'll be bigger.

MARIE BARRETT: What's the biggest change you've made?

MARIE HARVEY: I used to be your age. Now I'm mine.

MARIE BARRETT: Are you going to Charleston for anything special?

MARIE HARVEY: Not special. No.

MARIE BARRETT: Just visiting?

MARIE HARVEY: Just divorcing. My divorce hearing is tomorrow.

MARIE BARRETT: Your family lives in Charleston?

MARIE HARVEY: Just my husband. Divorcing me isn't enough. He also needed to move to a different climatic region.

MARIE BARRETT: I'm sorry.

MARIE HARVEY: Don't be. We had ten happy years of marriage… which isn't bad out of twenty-five.

MARIE BARRETT: You were married that long?

MARIE HARVEY: Yeah, well, what's twenty-five years?

MARIE BARRETT: Me. My birthday was last month.

MARIE HARVEY: Well I hope the past twenty-five years have brought you more happiness than they've brought me.

MARIE BARRETT: I don't know that they have.

MARIE HARVEY: Unless the only things you have to show for them are bills from your lawyer and a tan line on your ring finger, I'd say they have.

MARIE BARRETT: Are those really the only things you have? Bills and—?

MARIE HARVEY: And in a couple of weeks I won't even have a tan line.

MARIE BARRETT: You don't have any children?

MARIE HARVEY: I didn't say that.

MARIE BARRETT: Oh. So you do have something.

MARIE HARVEY: Divorces don't allow for much neutrality. At least not in my family. Good news is, if you know anyone at Hallmark, you can tell 'em to make one less Mother's Day card this year.

[MARIE BARRETT *stares sympathetically at* MARIE HARVEY. MARIE HARVEY *tries to ignore her for as long as she can and then:*]

MARIE HARVEY: Yes?

MARIE BARRETT: If you want to talk about anything, I'm a great listener. I wouldn't mind at all. Really. I don't know much about divorce, but I know a lot about being alone. Would you like to talk about being alone?

MARIE HARVEY: Not at the moment. Maybe when we reach cruising altitude.

MARIE BARRETT: Well you know where to find me.

[MARIE BARRETT *returns to her book.* MARIE HARVEY *tries to read her magazine, but keeps looking at* MARIE BARRETT *as if she wants to say something.*]

MARIE HARVEY: Um… excuse me—

MARIE BARRETT: Yes?

MARIE HARVEY: Nothing, I'm sorry.

MARIE BARRETT: No, no. Did you want to talk about something?

MARIE HARVEY: No. I—

MARIE BARRETT: Go ahead. I'm listening.

MARIE HARVEY: It's just, well, I can't help it, the mother in me wants to tell you to turn the light on while you're reading.

[*A call button "bing" is heard, indicating a "passenger" requesting service.*]

MARIE BARRETT: What did you say?

MARIE HARVEY: You should turn the light on. You're destroying your eyes—

MARIE BARRETT: No, no before that. What did you say before that?

MARIE HARVEY: Nothing.

MARIE BARRETT: No. Something. "The mother in me." Right?

MARIE HARVEY: Yeah…

MARIE BARRETT: That's what I thought. Wow.

MARIE HARVEY: What?

MARIE BARRETT: Wow.

MARIE HARVEY: What?!

MARIE BARRETT: I'm just going to seize the opportunity, OK? Because who knows when it will ever come my way again.

MARIE HARVEY: I don't know what you're talking about.

MARIE BARRETT: I'll throw out a bunch of questions and you can answer them one at a time… or pick and chose the ones you want—whatever feels right… Just go wherever "the mother" in you takes you, OK? All right, this is it.

[*Taking a deep breath.*]

Would you definitely say it's better to breast-feed a baby? Does the fork go on the left or the right? Um… oh yeah—is it true you can't wear white until after Memorial Day? And should you really wait an hour after eating to swim? Um… damn, why haven't I been writing these down? I literally have hundreds—*thousands* of—Oh, I know, if an invitation says "and guest"—

MARIE HARVEY: I just thought you should turn your light on.

[*She reaches above* MARIE BARRETT'*s head and turns on her light.*]

That's all.

MARIE BARRETT: I know you must think I'm a weirdo, but I'm not.
I don't have a mother, you see. It's something I'm aware of every second of the day. Like if I didn't have any arms or legs... or skin. She
died during childbirth. They say as soon as I emerged—as soon as I
took my first breath, she took her last. She really was only a vessel for
me if you think about it—just like this plane. She received me, took
me to a destination and then I emerged, disembarked and she was gone.
Lame metaphor I know, but the mind—my mind—needs ways to
understand, to make sense. I'm always feeling so... lost—like everyone in the world has a map that I don't have. Sometimes, I find I just
don't know how to get around. Like there's vital information I don't
have access to. Letters missing from my alphabet, you know? But now,
all of a sudden... here you are. I know this is lousy timing given your
situation, but there's too much I need to know. So I'm just gonna grab
a hold of this before it floats away. OK?

MARIE HARVEY: I don't think so.

MARIE BARRETT: But you offered—

MARIE HARVEY: I didn't offer anything.

MARIE BARRETT: Yes you did.

MARIE HARVEY: No I didn't.

[*Beat.*]

MARIE BARRETT: How many children did you say you have?

MARIE HARVEY: I didn't.

MARIE BARRETT: Sons?

[MARIE HARVEY *shakes her head "no."*]

Daughters. How many?

MARIE HARVEY: Enough.

[MARIE HARVEY *flips through her magazine. Pause.*]

MARIE BARRETT: My name's Marie. What's yours?

[*No response.*]

OK—I'll guess.

MARIE HARVEY: [*Before she can guess.*] Marie.

MARIE BARRETT: Yes?

MARIE HARVEY: No. That's my name too. Marie.

MARIE BARRETT: Is that the truth? Is it?

MARIE HARVEY: Yes.

MARIE BARRETT: That's… phenomenal. My God! Can you believe it? Maybe that's how they seat us.

VIRGINIA: Ladies and gentleman, the pilot has just turned off the fasten seat belts sign indicating that you are free to move about the cabin.

MARIE HARVEY: [*Unfastening her seat belt.*] Hallelujah.

MARIE BARRETT: It's an amazing coincidence, don't you think?

VIRGINIA: However, for your safety, we recommend you keep your seat belt fastened while you are seated. Also, please remember that due to Federal regulations, smoking is not permitted on this flight. If you choose not to obey these rules, you all might not get that midday snack you were promised. Just a joke. We will be around shortly with our complimentary beverage service. Please refer to the "Flight" magazine in the seat pocket in front of you for your selections. Thank you.

MARIE BARRETT: Marie, there's something I really need to ask you—

MARIE HARVEY: Look, I don't know you—

MARIE BARRETT: My name is Marie Barrett. I live in Brooklyn, I'm 25 years old, I'm Episcopalian. I work for a small but reputable publishing company and... um... I'm allergic to birch trees. What else do you want to know?

MARIE HARVEY: I shouldn't have said anything about the light.

MARIE BARRETT: The mother in you couldn't help it.

MARIE HARVEY: Marie, in twenty-four hours I have to stand in front of a judge and a bunch of other strangers and bicker with my husband about how much of an allowance he'll give me per month so at forty-nine years old, and having acquired no marketable skills, I won't have to beg anyone to give me my first job—

MARIE BARRETT: You've never had a job?

MARIE HARVEY: I paint.

VIRGINIA: Hello, ladies. What would you like to drink today?

MARIE BARRETT: [*To* MARIE HARVEY.] You paint? I work for a children's book publisher. I could help you find a job.

MARIE HARVEY: [*To* VIRGINIA.] Are there any empty seats?

MARIE BARRETT: Please don't.

VIRGINIA: No ma'am, there are no vacancies. And as far as I can tell, that seat you got there is perfectly fine, so let's not make complaints just to hear the sound of our own voices, OK?

MARIE BARRETT: Is your name Marie?

VIRGINIA: No. It's Virginia. Why?

MARIE BARRETT: We're both Maries.

VIRGINIA: Really? Isn't that an amazing coincidence?

MARIE BARRETT: It sure is.

VIRGINIA: So. What can I get you two Maries to drink?

MARIE BARRETT: Orange juice please. Wait. No. My stomach feels a little weird. All this excitement's got it doing somersaults.

[*To* MARIE HARVEY.]

Is it OK to have the acid? What does the mother in you say about that?

[MARIE HARVEY *does not respond. She continues to flip through her magazine.* VIRGINIA *and* MARIE BARRETT *stare at* MARIE HARVEY *for a few beats.*]

VIRGINIA: Ma'am?

MARIE HARVEY: What?

[MARIE HARVEY *realizes they are staring at her.*]

VIRGINIA: What's your call on the OJ?

MARIE HARVEY: Oh good God—have ginger ale.

MARIE BARRETT: Excellent. Ginger ale please.

VIRGINIA: Peanuts?

[MARIE BARRETT *and* VIRGINIA *look at* MARIE HARVEY, *as if asking her a question.* MARIE HARVEY *sighs heavily.*]

MARIE HARVEY: Are they salted?

VIRGINIA: Yes.

MARIE HARVEY: Skip the nuts.

VIRGINIA: And what would you like for yourself?

MARIE HARVEY: A Bloody Mary.

[VIRGINIA *looks at her watch.*]

Believe me, I'm entitled to it today.

MARIE BARRETT: She certainly is. Her divorce hearing is tomorrow.

VIRGINIA: [*Sympathetic.*] Do you really think alcohol is an answer?

MARIE HARVEY: No. Alcohol is a beverage. You asked me if I wanted one and that's the one I chose.

VIRGINIA: Suit yourself. But remember, I do have the authority to cut you off at any time.

MARIE HARVEY: Don't worry, I found a designated driver to fly the plane.

VIRGINIA: I'm only doing my job. Four dollars, please.

MARIE HARVEY: I don't suppose I can start a tab.

VIRGINIA: That's not in keeping with our policy.

[MARIE HARVEY *pays her.* VIRGINIA *pours ginger ale into a glass.*]

When I was a little girl, and my tummy felt funny, my mother would stir up my ginger ale until all the bubbles were gone.

MARIE BARRETT: Oh yeah? Why?

VIRGINIA: Strangely enough, I never asked.

[MARIE BARRETT *looks at* MARIE HARVEY.]

MARIE HARVEY: I am not stirring your ginger ale.

VIRGINIA: Would you like me to stir it for you?

MARIE BARRETT: Yes please.

[VIRGINIA *stirs and then stops suddenly.*]

VIRGINIA: Whoops. There's no tomato juice on my cart. Be right back.

[VIRGINIA *hands* MARIE HARVEY *the ginger ale and walks to the front of the plane.* MARIE HARVEY *looks at ginger ale for a moment, sighs heavily and then begins to stir.*]

MARIE HARVEY: It prevents gas.

[MARIE HARVEY *hands* MARIE BARRETT *the ginger ale. A call button "bing" is heard.*]

MARIE BARRETT: Thank you.

[MARIE BARRETT *sips her ginger ale and watches* MARIE HARVEY *read her magazine.*]

Could I ask you just one thing? Just answer this one question and then you can go back to your magazine, which I can tell you're only *pretending* to read. Marie? Could you put that down, please? Please?

MARIE HARVEY: Are you working for my husband? Did he hire you to drive me mad?

[VIRGINIA *returns, handing* MARIE HARVEY *a Bloody Mary.*]

VIRGINIA: You sip this slowly now, understand?

[*Pointing to* MARIE BARRETT's *glass.*]

Did you stir that for her?

MARIE HARVEY: Yes.

VIRGINIA: Good. Lord knows I can't do it all.

[VIRGINIA *exits.* MARIE HARVEY *takes a big gulp of her Bloody Mary.*]

MARIE BARRETT: I wouldn't bother you like this if I hadn't been waiting what feels like my whole entire life to ask someone this quest—

MARIE HARVEY: In approximately five minutes, this Bloody Mary will kick in, allowing me to pretend I don't have to do tomorrow what I have to do tomorrow. So if I enlighten you with some motherly advice now, you'll leave me alone for the rest of the flight, agreed? Minimal interaction only, right? Right?

MARIE BARRETT: Well, I might—

MARIE HARVEY: I'll sweeten the deal. Stop asking questions and the entire armrest is yours. OK? Maternal advice. Here goes—

[*Taking a drink.*]

If you *have* to get married, marry a lawyer... surround yourself with people you can tolerate but don't particularly like and most importantly—never, *never* have any children. Lovely meeting you—have a good trip.

[*She turns away.*]

MARIE BARRETT: Why shouldn't I have kids? Because I didn't have a mother of my own? Am I missing something essential that all other women have? Like some internal instruction book?

MARIE HARVEY: Just do what I did—read Dr. Spock and then hire a nanny.

[*She takes another gulp of her drink.*]

MARIE BARRETT: [*Laughs.*] Did your daughter inherit your sense of humor?

MARIE HARVEY: No, just my nervous condition.

MARIE BARRETT: I see.

MARIE HARVEY: You see? Really? What do you see? Do I have an "I've-driven-my-child-to-seek-extensive-psychotherapy" look to me? I've also driven her to an aromatherapist, a scalp masseuse, an herbalist, a dog psychologist...an astrologist...and a marriage counselor. And every goddamn one of them tells her it's all my fault.

MARIE BARRETT: Even the dog psychologist?

MARIE HARVEY: Apparently even little Snowcake isn't immune to the tension my visits create.

MARIE BARRETT: [*Laughs.*] You're really very funny.

MARIE HARVEY: Well, I'm glad you've enjoyed our little time together.

[*Lifting her glass in a toast.*]

Good-bye.

MARIE BARRETT: I have enjoyed it. That's actually what I wanted to ask you about. You see, I always hoped I could find someone…like you…who I could talk to from time to time. You know, like if I have any questions, maybe I could call you—

MARIE HARVEY: What?

MARIE BARRETT: I'm just so tired of never knowing where to find answers. I need someone…a woman…an older woman, who I can go to when I need help—

MARIE HARVEY: Are you asking me to be your mother?

MARIE BARRETT: No.

[*Beat.*]

It would be more like freelancing.

MARIE HARVEY: Good God—don't give yourself away to a stranger.

MARIE BARRETT: See—you're giving me advice already—you're a natural.

MARIE HARVEY: [*Uneasily.*] You're going too far. Now leave me alone.

MARIE BARRETT: I don't mean to imply that I'd call you constantly, just on occasion—

MARIE HARVEY: [*Overlapping.*] I'm not listening to this.

MARIE BARRETT: We both live in New York. We could meet for coffee from time to time.

MARIE HARVEY: Stop it.

MARIE BARRETT: Your own daughter would have first dibs of course, but we could all work out a schedule I'm sure—

MARIE HARVEY: Not another word.

MARIE BARRETT: Only when it's—

MARIE HARVEY: *I mean it!*

MARIE BARRETT: I'm sorry. This isn't a good time for you.

[MARIE HARVEY *finishes her drink, shakes the ice around her glass, then looks up and down the aisle.*]

I spend so much time trying to acquire family I can't imagine having to give any up. I'm sorry.

MARIE HARVEY: Don't be. My husband and I were happy for twenty years. And then we met.

[MARIE BARRETT *does not laugh.*]

MARIE HARVEY: [*Imitating a rim-shot.*] Ba-dump-ump.

MARIE BARRETT: Would you like to talk about how you're feeling?

MARIE HARVEY: I'm feeling annoyed.

MARIE BARRETT: I mean about your divorce. Would you like to talk about that?

MARIE HARVEY: Yes. But to someone I've known for longer than five minutes.

MARIE BARRETT: Well that's unfair.

MARIE HARVEY: What is unfair?

MARIE BARRETT: Shutting me out like that. It's not my fault we've only known each other for five minutes.

MARIE HARVEY: You shouldn't take it personally. I don't like talking to strangers.

MARIE BARRETT: Why?

MARIE HARVEY: Because they end up asking you to be their mother.

MARIE BARRETT: This has happened to you before? Has it?

MARIE HARVEY: I was speaking figuratively.

MARIE BARRETT: That's a relief. You're the first person I've asked. It would be just my luck if you had, like, a waiting list or something.

MARIE HARVEY: *I'm* the first person?

MARIE BARRETT: Yes.

MARIE HARVEY: Why on earth would *I* be the first person you've asked?

MARIE BARRETT: Because of what you said—"the mother in me." You saw me reading in the dark and the nurturer in you was so strong you couldn't resist reaching out to me. I'm a perfect stranger but you wanted to take care of me, to protect me. You're who I've been searching for. You've got the right stuff.

MARIE HARVEY: I don't have any stuff.

MARIE BARRETT: Exactly. You're alone like me. I mean, you're going to get divorced tomorrow, and no one's coming with you. It seems like… maybe…you have no one to ask.

[*Beat.*]

Hey—would you like me to go with you?

MARIE HARVEY: What?!

MARIE BARRETT: You don't want to be there alone, do you?

MARIE HARVEY: Thanks, but no thanks. Maybe next time.

MARIE BARRETT: I think you're looking for someone as much as I am.

MARIE HARVEY: Oh God, I'm in hell, I'm in sheer hell.

MARIE BARRETT: Truthfully, I don't believe for a second that you want me to stop talking to you.

MARIE HARVEY: Then make believe. Please.

[VIRGINIA *enters carrying plastic bags containing earphones. She passes them out to the other passengers.*]

VIRGINIA: Now don't y'all push these too far into your ears. With the cabin pressure being as high as it is, we don't want any of your heads exploding. Just a joke.

MARIE HARVEY: Excuse me—

VIRGINIA: [*Pointing at* MARIE HARVEY'*s empty glass.*] You shouldn't drink that fast.

MARIE HARVEY: I wouldn't drink at all if you could suggest another way to get it down.

VIRGINIA: Sarcasm will not get you better service.

MARIE HARVEY: I want to change my seat.

VIRGINIA: One at the bar perhaps?

MARIE BARRETT: Don't change your seat. I—

[*A call button "bing" is heard, indicating a "passenger" requesting service.*]

VIRGINIA: Duty calls.

[VIRGINIA *abruptly tosses* MARIE HARVEY *a package of headsets and quickly exits.*]

MARIE HARVEY: Hey!

[*She pushes the call button, but gets no response.*]

Oh, for crying out loud.

[*She rips plastic bag open, puts the earphones in her ears and stares out the window.*]

MARIE BARRETT: Please don't do that. I wasn't finished talking—

[MARIE HARVEY *closes her eyes and leans her head back.* MARIE BARRETT *stares at her.*]

I'm sorry to bother you, but there are things I have to talk to someone about. You see I'm really scared about something and there's no one else who I—Are you listening? Marie? Come on…Talk to me. I don't think what I'm asking is so bad…I only meant that I'd call you every once in awhile…just when I need an answer, or some advice. That's all, really. I just want to know there's someone out there I can talk to when I don't know what to do. Like about dating, or getting rid of strep throat…or cooking roasts…or buying flatware…or…or about…about lumps. You know, as in what if you feel something in your body you know wasn't there before?

[MARIE BARRETT *becomes more emotional.* MARIE HARVEY *removes her headsets and listens to her.*]

And you don't know a single thing about what a lump could be, except—And you're too scared to find out because you don't think you could go through anything that bad without someone…a mother to help you through it. Does it always mean something bad? Does a lump always mean cancer? Does it? Marie? Answer me. *Answer me please!*

[VIRGINIA *rushes over.*]

VIRGINIA: Is there something I can help with here?

MARIE BARRETT: [*To* MARIE HARVEY.] Does a lump always mean cancer?

VIRGINIA: Excuse me?

MARIE BARRETT: Does a lump always mean cancer?

VIRGINIA: Ma'am, I think I'll defer to you on that one.

MARIE BARRETT: Excuse me. I feel sick.

[*She exits to lavatory at the back of the plane.*]

MARIE HARVEY: Oh, brilliant. Is that how they teach you to handle crises in stewardess school? To defer?

[VIRGINIA *sits down in* MARIE BARRETT*'s seat.*]

VIRGINIA: Does she have cancer?

MARIE HARVEY: I don't know. She said she found a lump.

VIRGINIA: Does a lump always mean cancer?

MARIE HARVEY: Why is everybody asking *me* that?

VIRGINIA: Does it?

MARIE HARVEY: No.

VIRGINIA: Well, go on and tell her that.

MARIE HARVEY: I don't know who she is.

VIRGINIA: She seems to have formed an attachment to you.

MARIE HARVEY: Yes. However, I can't have her attached.

[*Beat.*]

Look, before she comes back, I need you—I *want* you to change my seat.

VIRGINIA: Tell her she's all right and then we'll discuss the seating arrangements.

MARIE HARVEY: I bought a ticket for this plane so I could get from point A to point B. That's it. As far as I know, I'm not required to adopt anyone. So move my seat, please.

VIRGINIA: That's against policy.

MARIE HARVEY: No it's not.

VIRGINIA: And how would you know? I don't see any wings pinned to your chest.

MARIE HARVEY: Don't force me to make demands—

VIRGINIA: Oh, we're threatening to make demands, are we? I guess our morning cocktail wasn't such a good idea after all, was it?

MARIE HARVEY: She won't leave me alone despite numerous requests—

VIRGINIA: Requests? No demands? I see, it's only airline personnel that are threatened with demands.

MARIE HARVEY: I apologize if I've offended you. I'm *asking* you, politely, could I possibly change seats with someone?

VIRGINIA: What would you like me to do? Walk up to a passenger and say, "Excuse me, that woman up there is sitting next to someone who is driving her crazy. Would you mind switching seats with her?"

MARIE HARVEY: Surely you can find another way to phrase it.

VIRGINIA: [*Earnestly.*] Go tell her she's all right.

MARIE HARVEY: I'd prefer it if you told her.

VIRGINIA: You know, I chose this profession so I could help people on a daily basis. But all it usually entails is passing out drinks and pillows. I know that. However, you have a real opportunity here to help someone. And for that I envy you.

MARIE HARVEY: If you want her, you can have her. She's currently accepting applications for a mother.

VIRGINIA: [*Patting* MARIE HARVEY's *lap.*] Not anymore. So. What kind of arrangement did you all work out?

MARIE HARVEY: We didn't work out an arrangement. She's a total stranger—

VIRGINIA: But "stranger" is a relative term. Compared to say, that gentleman right there, she isn't such a stranger, is she? You know her name, where she works… her current medical situation.

MARIE HARVEY: She's allergic to birch trees.

VIRGINIA: See there? Seems to me the two of you could have a nice little relationship.

MARIE HARVEY: There's no such thing as a nice little relationship.

VIRGINIA: Ma'am, I'm a recent divorcee myself, and personally the amount of people exiting my life is greater than the amount of people boarding, if you know what I mean. Lucky for you if that's not your situation. Oops, she's coming back. Try talking to her. You never know—

[MARIE BARRETT *returns to her seat.*]

How are you feeling, dear?

MARIE BARRETT: Fine, thank you. Could I have a pillow please?

VIRGINIA: Would you like a pillow also?

MARIE HARVEY: Just another Bloody Mary.

VIRGINIA: Are you su—

MARIE HARVEY: I'm sure.

VIRGINIA: [*To* MARIE BARRETT.] A lump doesn't always mean cancer, you know.

[*To* MARIE HARVEY.]

Does it?

MARIE HARVEY: No.

VIRGINIA: [*Indicating to* MARIE BARRETT.] Tell *her*.

[VIRGINIA *exits*.]

MARIE HARVEY: Are you OK?

MARIE BARRETT: Yes.

MARIE HARVEY: I'm sure there isn't anything wrong. But go to a doctor as soon as you get home.

[MARIE BARRETT *nods. Beat*.]

Usually, a woman your age has nothing to worry about.

MARIE BARRETT: Usually. The women in my family aren't really known for their longevity. So…I get scared.

MARIE HARVEY: [*Gently*.] Don't get so scared.

MARIE BARRETT: If this is bad, I won't be able to do it without…a mother.

MARIE HARVEY: I'm not who you want for a mother. The truth is, that's an item my own daughter is currently debating.

MARIE BARRETT: There's something unbelievable to me about a mother and a daughter not getting along.

CHICAGO PUBLIC LIBRARY
BEVERLY BRANCH
2121 W 95TH ST   60643

MARIE HARVEY: It's unbelievable to me that any do. If the truth be told, you've asked me more questions in the past ten minutes than my own daughter has asked me in the past ten years. I'm not as adept at mothering as you'd think.

MARIE BARRETT: I don't care. In fact, I prefer it that way. If you've been waiting ten years for someone to ask you for advice, you must have a lot of it to give. Right?

[MARIE HARVEY *laughs.*]

Hey, and just think, you'd be getting me at the best possible time. No teething, no toilet training…I've had all my shots.

[VIRGINIA *returns with a pillow and a glass.*]

VIRGINIA: Here's your *second* drink. FYI, regulations do not permit us to serve more than three.

MARIE HARVEY: Thank you.

[MARIE HARVEY *pays* VIRGINIA *for the drink.*]

VIRGINIA: My hands are full. Would you put this behind her?

[*Handing* MARIE HARVEY *the pillow.*]

[*To* MARIE BARRETT.] Lean forward honey.

[MARIE BARRETT *leans forward.* MARIE HARVEY *fluffs up the pillow and then puts it behind her.* VIRGINIA *watches happily.*]

So, is it settled? Are you two gonna go out and buy matching outfits?

MARIE HARVEY: Go away. Shoo.

VIRGINIA: Don't blow this.

MARIE BARRETT: You did tell me that all you have are lawyer bills and a tan line. When you said that, you reminded me of this quote I use to describe how I feel: "Life has not yet offered me a trinket of the slightest value." It's from Virginia Woolf—*Mrs. Dalloway*. Except for the yet. I added that—I try to be optimistic. "Life has not *yet* offered me a trinket of the slightest value." That's how you feel too, isn't it?

MARIE HARVEY: Well, like I said…I paint. That's my trinket.

MARIE BARRETT: [*Disappointed.*] Maybe I'll buy some watercolors.

MARIE HARVEY: I'm sure you have something.

MARIE BARRETT: Books, I guess. Virginia Woolf, Willa Cather, George Eliot. Anything written by a woman, I've read. But Virginia, Willa, and George, God bless 'em, have little to say about yeast infections and monthly mood swings. I can't find my mother in a book.

MARIE HARVEY: So now you're looking for her on airplanes?

MARIE BARRETT: I'm looking for her everywhere. I search for her the way you look for something you've dropped in the grass. Parting every blade…I used to dream that she didn't actually die. Instead a team of evil doctors kidnapped her from the operating table because she had a rare something or other—like three fallopian tubes. Or a five-chambered heart. I liked that idea the best—that she had a tremendous heart. Anyway, they kidnapped her to study her, so she's not really dead and it's only a matter of time until she escapes. And I find her… That's why I start conversations with strangers.

MARIE HARVEY: I don't have a tremendous heart.

MARIE BARRETT: How about three fallopian tubes?

MARIE HARVEY: I'm sorry. This arrangement you want, it's not possible.

MARIE BARRETT: Is there anything that could make it possible?

MARIE HARVEY: Marie, I need to get through the divorce tomorrow before I can think about any…acquisitions.

MARIE BARRETT: I understand.

CHICAGO PUBLIC LIBRARY
BEVERLY BRANCH
2121 W 95TH ST   60643

[*Beat.*]

Could I just ask you one more thing?

MARIE HARVEY: Yes?

MARIE BARRETT: A lump can really be something else besides cancer?

MARIE HARVEY: Yes. It can be just a cyst. Which I'm sure it is.

[*Beat. A call button "bing" is heard indicating a passenger requesting service.*]

Anything else?

MARIE BARRETT: What's a duvet?

MARIE HARVEY: It's like a giant pillowcase—for a comforter. When you want a new look.

MARIE BARRETT: Does it hurt to breast-feed a baby?

MARIE HARVEY: It sort of feels like jogging without a bra.

MARIE BARRETT: Will I ever enjoy sex as much as the man?

MARIE HARVEY: Probably not. But sometimes.

MARIE BARRETT: What's parboiling?

MARIE HARVEY: It's when you boil something for a short time—to pre-pare it for roasting.

[*Lights begin to fade.*]

MARIE BARRETT: I keep getting canker sores on my gums.

[MARIE HARVEY *maternally inspects* MARIE BARRETT'*s gums.*]

VOICE OF PILOT: Ladies and gentlemen, this is your captain. We're experiencing some minor turbulence. Please remain in your seats with your seat belts fastened while we find you a smoother ride.

[MARIE BARRETT *and* MARIE HARVEY *fasten their seat belts.*]

MARIE HARVEY: You probably have too much acid in your diet.

[*Fade to black.*]

<u>END OF PLAY</u>

CHICAGO PUBLIC LIBRARY
BEVERLY BRANCH
2121 W 95TH ST   60643